DIALOGUE

ON

DR. TEMPLE'S ESSAY,

WITH PREFACE

IN

Reference to the Recent Sermon and Speech

OF THE

LORD BISHOP OF EXETER.

By J. N. D.

London:

W. H. BROOM, 28, PATERNOSTER ROW.

—

(*Price Two Shillings.*)

Butler & Tanner,
The Selwood Printing Works,
Frome, and London.

PREFACE.

The following review of Dr. Temple's paper in the "*Essays and Reviews*" was published shortly after that volume appeared.

Circumstances with which every one is familiar have given occasion to its now appearing by itself. Dr. Temple does not intend to republish his Essay, but he has declared, if we are to accept his reported statement, that he retracts nothing, and that he pronounces no judgment on the other papers in the volume of "*Essays and Reviews.*" It is not his place to do it.

Now it is admitted that there is a difference, as stated by the Right Reverend Prelate, between an Essay of Frederick Temple and a paper from one in his present position. Quite true. But put the case :—I come to one I know and tell him, Those two persons I saw you with, as companions, were making and maintaining the most villanous statements as to your mother and her character. He replies to me, "The free handling" of character "in a becoming way" is useful to society : there may be mischief from it, but on the whole it is an advantage : it is not my place to judge every word and expression of my friends, nor am *I* responsible for what *they* say. I pronounce no opinion, it is not my place. I reply, *But* they were speaking of your mother : no word does the mouth proffer—no heart to suggest, to force that word.

Christ is outraged, dishonoured, blasphemed—His truth denied—direct association with that is out of place for office. But Christ! Is the dishonour to Christ and to the Word of God unfelt? I have no pretension to counsel a Prelate of the Establishment, but a Christian may ask, may wonder that the heart of Frederick Temple should feel nothing in these *Essays* that should draw forth some word that the dignity of office could not hinder. In this respect the reported speech in Convocation is sorrowful in the last degree. Official propriety is safe; and Christ—where is He? And it must be allowed me to add that the question is not at all that on which Dr. Temple enlarged—the advantage or disadvantage of free enquiry. Minds may differ as to that, but the free enquiry will go on in spite of me or Dr. Temple either. But in the Essays this is not the subject, nor are they even enquiry itself, but, save some brighter gleams of spiritual cravings in Dr. Jowett, the elaborately and diligently wrought effort of the infidel side in the enquiry. I ask any one who has read them if this be not so ; if that for which a Prelate in Convocation has not a word of approval or blame is not diligently taught infidelity with scarcely any exception whatever ; and if Frederick Temple be merged in this office, has the Christian heart nothing to say?

It may be said, Why continue to review what is not to appear afresh? The answer is simple—His Lordship has expressly declared that he means no retractation; *that* widely dispersed, as every one knows, and no retractation meant nor condemnation of what originally accompanied it; the judgment of what it is is perfectly legitimate therefore.

It is important it should be felt that it is not the fact of free inquiry which is in question. That may be anxious search for truth; or it may be the carnal will seeking weapons of enmity against God. What is in question is, with small exception, the elaborate adoption of the infidel side in the inquiry. But outside the dull monotony or bigoted imposition of ecclesiastical tradition and the wild claims of man's intellect to call everything in question, or scan everything by its own powers—the folly of ever-varying unbelief that finds no end—there lies divinely given but intelligent faith in the Word of God. The sober and lowly conviction that God has acted towards us in grace and has given a revelation which is not the activity of our minds, but acts through grace on mind and heart and conscience; a conviction which recognises with far greater intelligence than infidelity that it is not merely the activity of man's mind that is the source of truth (for it *never* is), but that God can act by His truth on the mind, on the whole moral being, making Himself known; and this acquaintance with divine revelation makes Christ's person, and Christ's work, and the Word of God itself, more precious than a mother's love, sweet and powerful as that may justly be; for nature gives them a power which is above the conventionalities of office and the influence of early and human associations.

It is not for me to judge how far Dr. Temple professes this. Not only as a Christian ought I to hope all things, but from his sermon at Exeter, though there was a fatal absence of redemption in it, one cannot but trust that the Word of God and person of Christ have hold upon his soul. But till we know redemption we never know ourselves, nor can there be that value for the Son of God, the Saviour, which rises, and raises us, above the motives and habits of the scene in which we move, and, if we all fail in detail, still we can say, above the pretensions and weaknesses of poor fallen human nature. Of this, Dr. Temple's discourse in Convocation, as reported to us, does not testify; and it is a fair and just service to enquire into the value of that which is professedly not retracted.

The Review is republished as it was years ago, with only such corrections, in stops and the like, which were found necessary on reading it over. If some feeling be expressed under the impression produced by the "*Essays and Reviews*," certainly no want of charity towards individuals is intended; and the expression of feeling has its right place.

CHRISTIANITY

AND THE

EDUCATION OF THE WORLD.

WELL, *H.*, have you read the "Essays and Reviews"?

H. I have; I am somewhat late in doing so; I thought I might have seen them abroad, but the book was not sent to me as I expected. But my sojourn there has enabled me to judge somewhat more distinctly of the character of this effort. As might be supposed, it is not an isolated one in the remarkable working of principles, both good and evil, which we see in the present day.

W. You do not mean that rationalism is on the increase in Germany (I think you were last in that country).

H. By no means. It had found the extreme of its limits both religiously and philosophically, and the reaction has necessarily set in: for truth there is, and good there is, at least in God, in spite of man; and when men have displayed the extremes to which the evil of human nature and human will and its revolt against God can go, there is, under divine light (at least till man, as we read, be given up to believe a lie) a reaction of natural conscience, and the instinct which knows and feels that a God there is, and that He is and must be good. Under this influence man revolts against what shocks a conscience informed by Christianity, and in a general way, desires to have to say to God, because he has learned that He is good, and feels that a bad God, a God with whom

B

we have nothing to do, and a revelation that is only deceit and falsehood, can give no comfort.   I have no thought that a man can go right without grace; but there is a natural conscience which sees through dishonesty, and wants truth and grace—sees, at least, that the contrary is not a true representation of God.   It wants something more sure in a revelation than a product of a man's mind, a history of the Hebrew monarchy, or an inspiration somewhat, perhaps, superior to Shakspeare, which learned men can criticise.   This may do for Essayists and Reviewers, but it will not do for the wants of the soul in daily life.   It will not do for the poor.   Such views may make pretentious infidels of them, retailing what they have read, and thinking themselves wise, because they have a certain number of objections against what is good and blessed; but they can give no help or food to any. I have always remarked of infidels, or infidel writers (for it is better to call things by their names), that they can make you doubt (no wonder) of many things, but they can give you nothing.   They never give you one certain truth.   The word of God gives you many certain truths. It makes you doubt of nothing.   It has no need; for it possesses the truth, and gives what is positive.   This is an immense difference : it stamps both morally.   When infidel minds speak of a love of truth, they never, that I can see, go farther than Pilate : What is truth?   It is never a holding fast truth they have got, but a casting doubt on what others believe, and, professing to search for it, always to be ready to receive it, I suppose because they have never got it.

W. But when you speak of the wants of the soul, do you believe that in the mass of men these spiritual wants exist?

H. I believe there are hidden wants everywhere. I do not say a new nature, a changed will, but cravings of a soul that has capacities beyond the sphere in which it is imprisoned; rarely showing themselves in the toil and follies of life, but which press into notice on particular occasions through the disordered throng of thoughts which crowd the avenues and people the busy interior of a dissipated and care-burdened existence. But it is not of this I speak now. I think that the mass of the poor have more reality of thought than reasoners,—see more justly the true character of things. The occupation with labour gives this. They toil to exist. That is now God's ordinance. What they get outside it must be real. Speculation has no place here. They may know nothing of a revelation, but if they have the thought that there is one, they want one that is a revelation from God—something He has told them, not an improved Shakspeare. If they have Diana and Jupiter, they take Diana and Jupiter as realities. If they are under the law of Moses, they will not spiritualize everything with Philo, or his modern imitators. They will take it as Moses gave it, or not at all. If they are idolators, they will be idolators *bonâ fide*, not readers of Lucian. If they are sceptical—if this pervades the population—not merely religion, but the state is near its 'end. By that I mean society. When man speculates on the sanctions of social life—when the divine ever-living power of faith is gone, that holds man subject to something superior to himself—when what links man to man is gone, self is dominant, conscious that it is self. A few minds may speculate on how much may be true, and seek refined notions out of the condemned mass of materials : the mass of men will be indifferent to all. Despotism or anarchy ensues. How long did the Roman empire survive Lucian, who was but a sign of the times? or the French monarchy the Encyclopedists? On the fall of Rome Christianity came in as a bond; now I see not what will, save the faithfulness of God and the Lord Himself from heaven. This does not prove that anything is true, I admit; but it proves that there is moral power in faith, and that the absence of faith is the destruction of society. And upon the face of it, the faith of the masses is not discriminative speculation.

W. But are you one of those who take religion to be a means subservient to society?

H. God forbid. The revelation of God is, for me, the putting an immortal soul, through grace, in communication with the eternal fountain of blessedness, of light, of love—with God Himself. Doubtless, most important revelations accompany it, necessary for the existence or full development of this. I have God manifest in the flesh. I have the blessed relationships of Father, Son, and Holy Ghost, without which it is impossible for man to be thus connected with God. Besides, I have the Church united to Christ—subjects into which I cannot enter now, but which (while, when revealed, they give to us conscious links of union with what is divine, and develop divine affections in the relationships they place us in) must be the subject of revelation. Man's mind cannot go beyond its own sphere. It is not God, and, if it is to be really elevated, must be elevated by something that is outside and above itself. That is, there must be a positive revelation of something not within the sphere of its own proper apprehensions. It may develop its own powers, it may create poetically what is within the sphere of those powers; but in the nature of things it cannot by itself get beyond itself. You may have Shakspeare to give all the scope of the human mind, all its workings, in a course of pictures, from its highest to its lowest forms, with a graphic truth which may interest in the most absorbing way minds inferior to his—minds which cannot do this for themselves; but it is always and must be the human mind, and within the sphere of its own limits, or it would not be the human mind. The consequence is that, though it may elevate these inferior minds above their level, it contents them with man, and in result, by excluding God, degrades them from what they might be. Poetry is the effort of the human mind to create, by imagination, a sphere beyond materialism, which faith gives in realities. But then it cannot rise above the level of its source, whatever displays of force there may be by its being conducted in a secret channel, and not exposed to be wasted in the open intercourse of the world. In result, it sinks down to the level towards which all human nature runs, and then settles, not to rise again. There may be a certain subjective development of mind in its use, but no more.

W. But men speak of the inspiration of Shakspeare and others—even of ordinary men, under happy or religious influences.

H. There is a confusion of language and thought between revelation and inspiration. We may use the latter term figuratively of the animated efforts of the human mind, compared with the platitudes of ordinary life, or, as is habitually done, of the instrumental power by which unknown truths are communicated by God to the human mind. But revelation is quite another thing, of which inspiration in the highest sense is but the form or instrument (for it is both)—that is, the actual presentation to us of an object, or a truth, or a fact not otherwise known. Here I get an additional object not otherwise obtained for the human mind.   As to will, moral or spiritual qualities, the mind may or may not be capable of discerning or appreciating it.   That is a theological question, a most important one, but not exactly our topic now.   But revelation is the declaration, the actual promulgation, of otherwise unknown truths—often those which could not otherwise be known.   Sometimes of those which in the actual condition of the individuals could not be known.

There is another enormous moral mistake,—that internal power is that by which man advances in the moral scale of being.   Power in man is limited to what man is.   That is no advance beyond what he is.   An acorn may become an oak, but in its nature it is never but an oak.   Even so power is not the real thing that elevates man (though in man there is another question: an oak is not a corrupt fallen thing).   "I can do all that may become a man; who can do more is none."   There is man's power at its limit.   If I may quote one who amongst men had hardly his like, I find more; I only say now, he pretends to more; let history and facts judge of his claim :—"I can do all things through him that strengtheneth me."   Here I find another and divine source of strength carrying him morally beyond man.

But (to state to you distinctly the principle I refer to) a dependent being (and a creature is a dependent being or a revolted one, perhaps a revolted dependent one) is elevated by its wants, not by its powers.   Its powers may develop it, but cannot elevate it.   But if I have a want, which is not power, and there is that which meets my want outside myself, I become acquainted with it.   I appreciate it, not by power, but by dependence on the quality by which my want is supplied.   Hunger is not power; but it enjoys and appreciates food which gives power.   Weakness is not power; but if my languid body leans on kindly and supporting strength, my felt weakness makes me know what strength is. But I learn more by it. I learn the kindness, patience, goodness, readiness, help, and perseverance in helping which sustain me. I have the experience of independent strength, adapted, suited to my weakness. I know its capacity to sustain what is beyond itself, which is not my power elevating itself in internal development—self-filling power. There is love.

Now this relationship of wants to that which supplies them in another is the link between my nature and all the qualities of the nature I lean on, and which supplies these wants. I know its qualities by the way it meets my not having them—my want of power. It is a moral link too. I know love by it, and all the unfolding of goodness; self-power never does. The exaltation of what is human in itself is the positive loss of what is divine, that is, infinite positive loss. There is immense moral depth in the apostle's word: When I am weak, then am I strong. And the more I have of God, and the more absolutely it is so, the more I gain. All is appropriated, but self is destroyed. It is not that I cease to exist, or to enjoy. It is not a Buddhist or stoical pantheistic absorption into God. I am always the conscious I for ever; yet an I which does not think of I, but of God in whom its delight is. It is a wonderful perfection—an absolute delight in what is perfect, but in what is perfect out of ourselves, so that self is morally annihilated, though it always is there personally to enjoy. This is partly now in the form of thirst, though there be enjoyment—hereafter, for those who have it, perfect enjoyment face to face. God alone is sufficient for Himself, is αὐτάρκης, and hence not self-seeking, for that comes from not being satisfied, not sufficient 'for self. Out of Him the αὐτάρκεια is pride, satisfaction with misery, and itself a sin; dependence is the right, holy, loving, excellent place. To be independent, if we are not God, is folly, stupidity, and a lie,— living in a lie. If we are God, we must be the only one, or we are it not at all. Yet in Christianity we are made partakers of the divine nature, in order to our having the fullest capacity of enjoyment; but for that very reason we have (He being perfectly revealed) such a knowledge of Him as makes us undividedly delight in His infinite excellence, and makes our independence to be our deriving in love from infinite excellence, and in our normal state unmingled delight in it.

The connection of the derivative and perfect objective character of divine life and love is what is so brought out in John, particularly in his epistle; it makes its essential depth and beauty, and, when not seized because not possessed, its difficulty and apparently mystic character. It is this which makes the Trinity have so sure and perfect a place to the soul. I do not use this as a proof, save as the real present enjoyment of anything proves to the heart it is true. In the Father I have absolute Godhead in its own intrinsic permanent perfection. In the Son I find what is divine (if not in the same perfection, I have not God revealed) brought out in man, fully wrought into all that is sinlessly human; so that it is not only suited to man but to be apprehended (if morally capable of it) by man. *All the fulness* of the Godhead dwells in Him bodily, at the same time in the personal relationship of Son. And the Holy Ghost (besides my having a life from God, and so being partaker of the divine nature) is the power in me (morally as well as in power of apprehension) by which I apprehend and enter into communion with God, with the Father and the Son; while this presence of the Holy Ghost secures in my feebleness the truth and purity of this communion, because any inconsistency grieves Him; and He works in the conscience by the revelation of God, though not then in communion.

Now you must see that there is much that must be directly revealed in such subjects as these. Even of what is bodily brought before us, as in the life of Jesus on earth, though in itself a revelation, an account of it is needed, not only to perpetuate it—which is quite true—but also to give a divine view of the thing revealed, which, it is evident, man by sight would have hardly seized in its full extent or bearings; or could not in its links with other unseen or unknown things. But besides this, we want a divine account of what is short of the revelation of God Himself to man; namely, a revelation of the terms on which man stood with Him, and of His ways with man. This will involve man's imperfection, and, if historically given, the expression of that imperfection, but will be God's account of it.

W. Yes; but it is just when we get on this ground that there are difficulties and objections which perplex the mind—difficulties I mean both as to the record of truth, and as to the moral proprieties of evangelical truths.

H. I do not deny it; not that I judge they are very weighty. But as to the first point, it does not surprise me that, in a record which reaches over some fifteen hundred years or more, committed to the care of man—for that it professes to be—I should find the traces of the infirmity of man; while its state in those circumstances, and its whole history, is the most striking possible proof of the providence of God. It is of the essence of a revelation made in grace, to be adapted to man, connected with man, to pass through the medium of man's moral nature, and be put, so to speak, into his hands. It could not draw the sympathies of his nature in the same way if it did not. It would not associate man with God, if it did not connect God and man in interests, affections, moral nature, if it did not give a common ground of moral association. Hence the New Testament does it much more than the Old—is more familiar, more human, takes its place more in every element of human circumstances.

In the Old, after the revelation of the creation, as a starting-point and sphere of God's manifestation by and in man, I find history as to which I am left to judge morally—most instructive history, if I know how to use it; but a public government of this world, or occasional relationships between God and man, in which I have to form a spiritual judgment how far men are up to the height of a true association with God. For the true link was not yet formed by the full revelation of God in grace: only a partial revelation of it anticipatively, and particular communications; and God dwelt in the thick darkness: then oracular dicta, a "Thus saith the Lord"—God showing grace, speaking to man, but speaking Himself alone—no doubt by the mouth of men, His word using them so as to approach man in sovereign goodness where man had failed. The word of the Lord came to such a one it is said. But it was as an instrument, a channel of communication, so that they searched out the meaning of their own prophecies.

In the New, I find a history of perfection; for God is manifest in the flesh. It is not communications from a God not revealed, but the revelation of God. Hence it is perfect on His part in that association of which I spoke. It is the Word made flesh—God in man moving in the circumstances of men amongst men, and is not what I have to judge of spiritually in man, but the perfection which judges all else—the truth, an object, which, if I have a heart capable of seeing it and loving it, engages it absolutely, because it is God, because it is man, because it is God in man, and I am a man; the perfect object linking itself with every moral delight of my new nature, meeting at the same time every want of my moral being in perfect grace; finding in those wants, yea, even in my sins, the occasion of manifesting grace to it, of making me know God by them—at least by the perception of the way He meets them in love. It forms and fills the capacities of my nature in what is divine, as beauty does a capacity to perceive it. Yet it meets all my wants with good, which puts man in his right place of dependence, in grace, on God; but gives entire confidence, because He is come as myself, as far as being a man in everything but what is a defect in man (that is, sin). He is that by which I judge everything, not which I have to judge as a history of man, though it be of man in various relationships with God.

Besides, I have in the New Testament, another immensely important element of our relationship with God. This blessed One was rejected. Such is the history we have. It is the full discovery of this solemn truth, that the carnal mind is enmity against God. And the other part of the New Testament is the unfolding of the way in which, through God's being sovereign in love over man's evil, He has, in the perfect display of righteousness, been able—glorifying Himself perfectly in the work of Christ in the putting away of evil—to associate man in his new nature with Himself, out of the reach of the evil, and according to His own perfection, where the feebleness and the misery will and can exist no longer. Thus a perfect heavenly relationship is formed, ourselves holy and without blame before Him in love, and His own children in His house, associated with and like Him who became a man for us in grace. To this are added the various exercises accompanying the knowledge and faith of this in weakness, and the fitting display of the fruits of it in those partakers of this life in connexion with heaven, but in the weakness of an earthly vessel. This display of the divine in man, and the bringing man up to God in His own blessedness, form the contents of the New Testament: we may add, the setting the world right ultimately, in peace, by the divine government in man.

What I have just remarked, if you examine it a little closely, you will find to be the difference between the writings of Paul and John, and the reason of the special attractiveness of the writings of the latter. John brings God down in man to earth. It is the divine down here, and it is the perfection of loveliness and truth. Paul brings man out of the earth and up to heaven. You will see that, save in casual allusions necessarily made or complementary to the main subject, John never takes even Christ up to heaven. He brings the divine person down here in human kindness, diffusing what is perfectly divine into the hearts of men that can receive Him, through his own person, and at any rate manifesting it among them. And hence too it is, that it was John's part to go on to the Apocalypse; because, though in certain respects on much lower ground, inasmuch as it is the government of the world, it is still the display of God's ways and character on the earth.

W. This to me, though thus briefly sketched, is profoundly interesting. But what place do the Psalms hold in this view of the character of the Old and New Testaments ?

H. I was going to say a word on them. They have their own and a very peculiar place. We have no devotional pieces prepared for the Church in the New Testament, which gives this point more importance, and I think additionally shows the grace of God, and the perfect and divine harmony of that book we call the Bible. I say, that book ; for, though there be many authors instrumentally, it is one book—though our *Bibliotheca Sancta,* as Jerome says.

In the New Testament the saints (having the knowledge of perfect divine favour, the love of God shed abroad in their hearts by the Holy Ghost given to them, and that blessed Spirit dwelling in them) are supposed to be capable of praising God freely. It is expressed in a very wonderful manner in Psalm xxii. After giving prophetic utterance to the sorrows of Christ, and His being forsaken of God, He is heard from the horns of the unicorn. As soon as He enters into the full light of His Father's countenance, according to the power of redemption and the work that He had wrought, He declares His Father's name, as He thus knows it, to His brethren : He puts them in relationship with the Father as He is Himself ; as He historically did, " Go tell my brethren . . . I go to my Father and your Father, to my God and your God." This was a position entirely new, consequent upon His resurrection, in which He had not only taken a new place as man, but acquired it for them. Then in the psalm He says, " In the midst of the church will I sing praise unto thee." Our praises then are the free and joyful following of Christ in the praises which He can raise, as man, in entering into the full light of His Father's countenance, according to the work He has wrought. But this could not be till perfect and intimate love was revealed to man, and men were brought, according to a righteous exercise of it, into the enjoyment of the light of God's countenance, according to the value of that work which had given them the title to be there.

Hence, if I should find the same perfection portrayed in the Old Testament as in the New, I should know it was not true. Before the revelation of God Himself, and our being brought on a new footing into His presence (that is, in the Old Testament), the dealings of God with man, on the moral condition in which he was as a child of Adam, are unfolded—God never leaving Himself without witness, for He is good, but for a time leaving man without an express revelation ; afterwards giving one of promise or of law, so that the moral nature of man should be wrought on by hopes, fears, promises, warnings, judgments, and mercies. In a word, God was dealing with man on the ground of man's responsibility, and trying the effect of motives. Could man in flesh, walking on the earth, be in relationship with God? It was not God Himself revealed, and man reconciled to Him according to His unclouded heavenly character, but God governing the earth in mercy and righteousness, and man's moral condition tested thereby: on the one hand, wickedness and self-will breaking forth, and, where there was really grace, failure no doubt, but faith in God, confidence, hope, integrity, acknowledgment of sin, dependence on and delighting in Him, in spite of all. But man, not being reconciled to God, knows God only by His ways, and a word adapted to man in this outside position. How, with failure and conscious sin, could that confidence be maintained, without which no heart-link could exist? If we are reconciled to God, where the Spirit of adoption is, when by one offering we are perfected for ever, praise is easy and spontaneous, though acknowledgment of failure be called for. If repeated sacrifices give momentary ease, yet even these were the witness that sin still subsisted. The way into the holiest was not yet made manifest; nor was God revealed outside it. He was a God of hope, not of communion.

Here the Psalms, in the most gracious and lovely way, find their place; not the peaceful breathings of a reconciled soul, but God furnishing the true but tried soul with divinely given and therefore surely accepted expressions of every feeling which a soul in such a state could need to express, and the witness of the entire sympathy of the Spirit of Christ in all their sorrows and exercises of heart. To be perfect, man must be within—children in a new accepted state. But for the heart divinely quickened, and exercised without—wishing, hoping, fearing, confiding, yet tried, guilty, sometimes almost despairing, yet still clinging—the Spirit of Jehovah puts His word in the tongue of the Psalmist to give a divine utterance to otherwise a perhaps distrusted feeling, or to draw the heart from a feeling of distrust: and the Psalms become the comfort of every tried and godly soul. Hence it is that, as the expression of a soul tried in the present dark government of this world, the judgment and destruction of enemies in this world is looked for—a judgment which must take place for the power of evil to be removed by government out of it. The Christian has nothing to do with that, because he is entirely associated with heaven, enters within the veil by a new and living way, and will leave the evil to go to heaven, and is above it morally all his life long.   Hence the thoughts and feelings of spiritual minds in the Old Testament must be imperfect.   They are the fruit of grace, giving confidence to the soul when yet far from God, and the expression of its feelings at that distance, and according to the state it finds itself in, looking to God in and out of that.   And all this I must have to know what the true condition of the human heart is, looked at in its exercised responsible condition out of paradise: man with a knowledge of good and evil; the goodness and righteousness of God as regards that state being revealed to him, and all the various workings of his nature under this provided for, with the promise of a better deliverance to come.   Christianity is another thing altogether: exercises there are, no doubt, but they are the exercises of a reconciled soul, which has its place and dwelling with God, known Himself in love.

W. But you do not feign that Old Testament saints looked only for temporal promises.

H. I do not.   I do not doubt that, according to the measure of their faith, though they did look for the exercise of God's government for deliverance here, yet in the delay of this they looked out of it all to a better place, though obscurely enough.   But this changes nothing. They looked to it as a resource out of a scene they belonged to.   The Christian dwells in it if in his right place, and has to cultivate the affections which belong to his Father's house as his own home.   You will remark that I do not merely mean that in result Old Testament feelings are imperfect, for that may well be said of ours; but that the basis of them, the moral sphere in which they moved, necessarily made them imperfect; they were not in place, if they were not.   God might inspire feelings right for those without—hope, desire, confidence; but He could not truly inspire to those without the feelings which expressed being within, for those feelings would not have been true. My feelings, if right, are the feelings of one within in my Father's house as a known home, reconciled to God. Theirs, if right, were those of persons without, looking for the present government of this world, and confiding in God in spite of subsisting evil in a world to which they belonged. He that is of the earth is earthy, says the greatest born of woman, and speaketh of the earth : He that cometh from heaven is above all ; and what He hath seen and heard that He testifieth.

W. I think I understand you ; but it was very great grace God's entering into the very sorrows and condition of an earthly people, at least, by His Spirit and word, furnishing them with assurances of His faithfulness, and expressions for a heart which could not speak as at peace, reconciled, and within, and yet needed the sense and sustaining of favour. Yet of course it is better to have affections which belong to the house developed within as children of the house. It gives a wonderfully interesting and enlarged scope of thought in reading Scripture, and makes God more familiar with the soul as truly estimating and dealing with its thoughts. But these saints will be in heaven ?

H. Doubtless they will. They received that Divine nature which has its place there, but not in the conscious heavenly relationship formed on known relationship. God had reserved some better thing for us, that they without us should not be made perfect. They will be made perfect in resurrection ; but what a lesson shall we have learnt,— ay, will the angels have learnt,—of the ways and dealings and goodness of God, and, instead of that miserable αὐτάρκεια, which was the heathen's boast, what a mould

ing of a thousand excellent feelings through dependence
on God, in the midst of evil and in the sense of imperfection, which He met by His word as a resource for faith!
How tender and familiar, while exalting His Majesty by
goodness, God thus becomes! Yet it was right we should
understand that by a perfect sacrifice we could in a new
nature enjoy God as He is in Himself, and that is our
Christian place. This is what the apostle unfolds in its
elements in Romans v. Being justified (for it must be a
Divinely righteous thing, or it is not really introduction
to God's nature) we have peace with God: as regards *all
evil* the question is settled; grace or favour wherein we
stand; our hope that of the glory of God Himself. These,
you would say, are all. Yes, as regards my place, but not
my exercises of heart. "Not only so, but we *glory* in
tribulations," not looking out of them merely in hope,
but glorying in them as a refining work, because the love
of God is shed abroad in our hearts by the Holy Ghost
given to us; and I have the key to all my sorrows: God's
love is the joy of my heart. Hence, again, not only so,
but I joy *in God*, through our Lord Jesus Christ, by whom
we have now received the reconciliation.

W. It makes rationalism and infidelity appear very
superficial.

H. There is nothing more characteristic of it than superficiality. It never gets beyond the bark and shell of
the Divine fruit of the word. In the midst of the most
admirable development of Divine ways, it will stop to
complain that the numberings of Israel and Judah are not
the same in Samuel and Chronicles. How, they ask me,
do you account for that? Suppose I answer (though in
this case there is not much difficulty) I cannot account for
it at all—I should not be a bit the worse off. I have a

positive proof of perfect Divine wisdom in the book and in all its details, for these details give to the whole the character it has. Man's estimate of things, partly influenced by the Spirit of God—his thoughts, his feelings, the evil, the rebellions, the faults, the unbelief, the way God met it—all go to make up the picture of what man was before God, and the scene of God's dealings in mercy and truth with men, till, as it is expressed, mercy and truth meet together, and righteousness and peace kiss each other. Every detail lost, would be a loss of the completeness. Some trait would fail of these wonderful unfoldings of what man is in relationship with God. Suppose my intelligence of some of the details fails me, that I cannot account for some phenomenon, I lose something of course —the proofs of the completeness. The dealings of God, however, have not disappeared. I cannot (I suppose the case) explain some particular point, nor solve an apparent discrepancy in a number. I pity the person whose perception of the perfection of all is hindered by a difficulty he cannot explain. To my mind the greatest part of these difficulties is the fruit of the ignorance and traditional views of the objectors. This volume proves it. I may not be able to solve, God may try our faith by, some such things, through the human weakness of those to whom these Divine oracles were entrusted; but He will always answer and bless our faith.

W. Have you any case on your mind?

H. I judge that superficiality is universally characteristic of rationalist views, but I will allude to one prominent subject with them. Before I heard of rationalists I had, as others no doubt, clearly seen the Petrine and Pauline and Johannean characters into which parts of the Divine revelation were thrown. Of the beauty and moral harmony, the goodness of God in this, the enormous gain and advantage to us, which fill the believer's mind, they have not the smallest perception. They can only spell out possible historical inconsistencies, and think of the books as the fruit of some ecclesiastical intrigues to reconcile Christian factions, or give the authority of apostolic names to cover resistance to heresies come in long after. That God in perfect love to man should give in one instruction how far the Christian, redeemed from the world, should, as a pilgrim in it, be connected with its government by God as more directly displayed in the Old Testament, as Peter does; that the blessed revelation of God Himself (as it is expressed, No man hath seen God at any time; the only-begotten Son, who is in the bosom of the Father, He hath declared Him) and of eternal life in Him in all its nature and qualities, should be given in John; and man presented to God in righteousness and resurrection, and conferred privileges in heaven, be developed in Paul :—all this is lost on them. They are trying to prove it imposture, or reconcile dates, or discuss the possible author, provided no one pretend it to be genuine. There is an incapacity to perceive the Divine which is difficult to conceive. Yet I believe it is useful. Happily the most advanced of these wise men are so entirely unhistorical, that they have no credit with sober minds, even with those who are not much affected by the Divine.

English theologians are so shut up in traditional lore, that they think rationalists have upset all inspiration, if they overthrow their own traditions; just as a poor Roman Catholic turns infidel often, if he comes to think a bit of bread is not the body, blood, soul, and Divinity of the Lord Jesus. Thus our Essayists tell us as a great discovery, that no man can now suppose that the tower of Babel was built to be high enough to escape the flood—a peurile conceit of which there is not a trace in the scriptural account, but, instead of it, an immense moral historical fact. Their declared object was to make themselves a name, to have a centre, which should hinder their being scattered abroad upon the face of the whole earth. It was centralization; not with God for a centre, but to combine the whole race in one system of united power. This God confounded, and made them into nations, which they had never been before at all. This immense fact in the history of the world they see nothing of, and think they have made a great discovery which upsets the Scripture account in showing that it could not be to escape the flood. "No doubt they are the men, aud wisdom shall die with them." We get in this part of Scripture the two great elements on which all the world has proceeded since—nationalities, and individual ambitions seizing imperial power. But you must never trust the statements of this class of persons as to anything. There is the greatest pretension to new light; and some very questionable hypothesis of a moment is stated as a settled ascertained fact, with a coolness which is a mark of the want of the honesty of a conscience fearing God. In those "Essays and Reviews" there are statements which are a disgrace to any upright or honest man —Jesuitical to a degree which is sufficient to destroy all moral confidence in one who could have such sentiments; the publication of which proves that those who publish them are arrived at a point of moral insensibility at which they have lost the sense of shame in making their shame known. They are not aware how bad it is.

W. But this is rather strong language.

H. To be sure it is; there are acts and traits in which,

if they do not excite indignation, one is a partaker morally. What do you say to this?—

"It is stated to be the affirming, that any of the Thirty-nine Articles are in any part 'superstitious, or erroneous.' Yet an Article may be very inexpedient, or become so; may be unintelligible, or not easily intelligible to ordinary people; it may be controversial, and such as to provoke controversy and keep it alive when otherwise it would subside; it may revive unnecessarily the remembrance of dead controversies— all or any of these without being 'erroneous;' and though not 'superstitious,' some expressions may appear so: such as those which seem to impute an occult operation to the sacraments. . . .

"The other canon which concerns subscription is the thirty-sixth, which contains two clauses explanatory, to some extent, of the meaning of ministerial subscription, 'That he *alloweth* the Book of Articles,' etc., and 'that he *acknowledgeth* the same to be agreeable to the word of God.' We 'allow' many things which we do not think wise or practically useful; as the less of two evils, or an evil which cannot be remedied, or of which the remedy is not attainable, or is uncertain in its operation, or is not in our power, or concerning which there is much difference of opinion, or where the initiation of any change does not belong to ourselves, either of the things as they are, or of searching for something better. Many acquiesce in, submit to, 'allow,' a law as it operates upon themselves which they would be horror-struck to have enacted; yet they would gladly and in conscience 'allow' and submit to it, as part of a constitution under which they live, against which they would never think of rebelling, which they would on no account undermine, for the many blessings of which they are fully grateful—they would be silent and patient rather than join, even in appearance, the disturbers and breakers of its laws. Secondly, he 'acknowledgeth' to be agreeable to the word of God. Some distinctions may be founded upon the word 'acknowledge.' He does not maintain, nor regard it as self-evident, nor originate it as his own feeling, spontaneous opinion, or conviction; but when it is suggested to him, put in a certain shape, when the intention of the framers is borne in mind, their probable purpose and design explained, together with the difficulties which surrounded them, he is not prepared to contradict, and he acknowledges. There is a great deal to be said, which had not at first occurred to him ; many other better and wiser men than himself have acknowledged the same thing—why should he be obstinate ? Besides, he is young, and has plenty of time to reconsider it ; or he is old, and continues to submit out of habit, and it would be too absurd, at his time of life, to be setting up as a church reformer. . . .

"We have spoken hitherto of the signification of subscription which may be gathered from the canons ; there is, also, a statute, a law of the land, which forbids, under penalties, the advisedly and directly contradicting any of them by ecclesiastics, and requires subscription with declaration of 'assent' from beneficed persons. This statute (13 Eliz. cap. 12), three hundred years old, like many other old enactments, is not found to be very applicable to modern cases ; although it is only about fifty years that it was said by Sir William Scott to be *in viridi observantiâ*. Nevertheless, its provisions would not easily be brought to bear on questions likely to be raised in our own days. The meshes are too open for modern refinements. For, not to repeat concerning the word 'assent' what has been said concerning 'allow' and 'acknowledge,' let the Articles be taken according to an obvious classification. Forms of expression, partly derived from modern modes of thought or metaphysical subjects, partly suggested by a better acquaintance than heretofore with the unsettled state of Christian opinion in the immediately post-apostolic age, may be adopted with respect to the doctrines enunciated in the first five Articles without directly contradicting, impugning, or refusing assent to them, but passing by the side of them—as with respect to the humanifying of the Divine word and to the Divine Personalities." —*Essays and Reviews*, pp. 182—186.

And remark here, this does not refer to minute discrepancies of view which are often connected with the very structure of individual mind where there is no real difference in substance. It is directly referred to the fundamental doctrines of the Incarnation and the Persons in the Trinity ; as to this they justify signing your assent, meaning that you do not agree, but "pass by the side of them." Now I say, that a person who could unblushingly avow such opinions does not deserve to be *heard on any* moral question whatever.

W. But you cannot charge them all with the views of one.

H. Not of course as to details; but when they agree to appear together, and bind up their articles in a common volume to act together on the public mind, by a common testimony, they are practically associated—I admit, not in details of opinions, but in the general purport and moral aim and character of the book. And I do say, that such pages as 180—186 put them out of court as to their title to be heard on Divine things.

W. They are very bad, in truth.

H. We will leave that, though to my mind it is not an evil that the minds of all who believe in the revelation God has given should know where the system of rationalism leads morally—at any rate, when it is attempted to be connected with established Christianity.

W. What were you saying as to the tendency you had observed on the Continent?

H. We have indeed had a long preface, but the perfect beauty of Scripture leads one on.

W. It is no loss to have had this much. I believe that the positive perception of the excellency and beauty of what is true and good is the best security against cavil and difficulties. These difficulties take their right proportion and their right place. The truth is Divinely certain. And there *are difficulties,* not objections.

H. Surely, and the difference is of all-importance. A person who makes an objection out of a difficulty proves the spirit he is animated with, especially when the thing he objects against is supremely lovely. He shows himself incapable of judging. Either he does not perceive the loveliness, or he dislikes it. But what you refer to was this, an effort to popularize, in France, as well as England, the infidel conclusions drawn from German research. I bought a translation of Job, by a first-rate oriental scholar in France, not heeding his opinions, but hoping to find some profound examination of the text. I found in his introduction merely the assumption, that all the German infidelity was a conceded matter, and putting it into plain French. This is just what the "Essays and Reviews" are attempting. Now where there is Divine faith, this does not do much; but the mass may have educational faith in the Scriptures, so that they are respected as true, and have a hold on the conscience. They cannot have by this the proof that the believer has, in that the word has Divinely reached his own conscience. But when the confidence of those who are believers in the word as such, by habit and education merely, is gone, you have to begin farther back in the matter; the population are tending to apostasy, not mere heart unbelief; and that is what Satan is seeking to do now. It is not the open honest denial of the old deist, against which the claims of a denied Christianity raised with most a rampart in the conscience too strong to be overcome; but the keeping up the name and garb of Christianity, and blunting its edge and undermining its foundations, so that what is of God in it may be wholly given up, and the authority of God's word over the conscience gone; for if it be God's word it has absolute authority. A man that would speak of Shakspeare having authority over my conscience would be a fool. They may parade human inspiration, and compare degrees of it. God's authority is wholly gone, and man is free in the perversion of his will. Shakspeare never made a saint. Modern infidelity will allow Christianity as much as you please, provided Christ be, as another, a minister to elevate humanity as it is—comes in His own place as one eminent instrument, and man, " I," be all.   I maintain the authority of God's word because it is God's, that man is lost in himself, and that God has appeared.   Owned, we possess Him in blessing; rejected, we are His self-condemned enemies.   I maintain redemption which brings man out of the condition he was in into another new and blessed one before God, according to His own righteousness and holiness.   I do not want humanity educated, but God known.

W. I see you have finished your preface, at any rate, and that your zeal has landed you at Rugby.   Let us hear what you have to say of Dr. Temple.

H. I am sure you will excuse my zeal.   I have not an unkindly feeling that I am conscious of towards a living being; but when I see what is Divinely perfect and good and reverenced flippantly assailed, I have no wish to exhibit indifference : and when men jeopard the faith of millions, as far as their acts are concerned, when they treat with a light hand the Lord of glory, and the authority of His words, they merit scornful rebuke for what they do, if even its execution be pretentious and superficial.

Such, whatever my feebleness in showing it may be, is the judgment I have formed of these " Essays and Reviews."   They are mischievous, not by their depth and seriousness, for they are neither deep nor serious ; but, as in a warehouse filled with oil, a spark that falls among shavings.   I agree with two Irish Archbishops, that they are dishonest, and with an English one, that they are very feeble.   But let us examine Dr. Temple on the education of the world.

The first thing that strikes me is, that there is no

glimpse or appearance of a thought of anything in man, but of the lower part of man—of man arriving as a race at a certain result down here in this world. God and a soul in connection with Him are altogether shut out. Supposing, what I do not believe, a succession of races, beginning and running through the same career in a succession of cycles, which is just the Platonic and Alexandrian idea; this would render, Dr. Temple tells us, the existence of each one of them unnecessary: the annihilation of a whole human race is absolutely nothing. Now as to progress in this world, or a development of man, as man merely, that is quite true. But what about the relationship of the souls which compose the race with God? Is that nothing? Or is that under the iron rule of a cycle which leads to no result? The supposition leaves out altogether every relationship between God and the soul. Redemption being an infinite thing in its nature, I do not believe there can be a repetition of such cycles, because I believe the Second Man is the *Last* Adam. Of course, this Christian doctor and instructor of youth does not trouble himself about redemption in his education of the world, nor will I here insist upon it; but if there were uniform cycles, and the result of each the same as to the public result, as to humanity in this world, the difference might be infinite as to everything of the highest nature in man, unless man is morally an absolute slave to the circumstances through which he passes. To say nothing of redemption, that is, God's actings about men, which makes the whole theory of the education of the world nonsense, the whole reasoning of Dr. T. excludes the idea of God and a *soul*.

W. Excuse me: he speaks of the effect on the souls of men in the second paragraph of his paper.

H. To be sure he does, and this is the clearest proof of what I say, and that it is true in the most offensive way. He says that, on the supposition of his uniform cycles, the lives and souls of men become so indifferent, that the annihilation of a whole human race, or of many such races, is absolutely nothing. Now this makes the souls of men absolutely nothing, but for a result of progress in this world. It goes so far that the soul's non-existence after death is absolutely indifferent; for their annihilation is nothing if progressive result as a race is not induced. And supposing the soul were not immortal, and were annihilated after death, the progress of the race could go on just as well; the succeeding generation would inherit the progress of the preceding, and go on towards the ultimate result. Those that were dead need not exist *at all* for that.

W. Yes, my friend, but there is an aspect of this you have not considered; it may be alleged that the doctrine of the immortality of the soul is necessary for this progress.

H. Excuse me, my dear W.; I have considered it. Either the doctrine of the immortality of the soul is true, or it is not (and the doctrine itself proves the doctrine true). If it be not true, I have, on the supposition you make of its being used, an imposture which involves considerations leaving this poor world and its progress in the shade of nothingness, used for the sole purpose of leading the race to progress, as its result—a use which makes the immortality absolutely nothing—which is really as absurd as it is false and dishonest; or immortality and the all-important considerations which accompany it are true; and they make the progress of the race a mere accident comparatively, and all Dr. Temple's views miserably false, to the shame of one who could have held them. No, he has a world without souls, and souls without God.

W. I see you have considered it, and what you say is true. It is evident that this system ignores (or worse) God, and all the higher parts and relationships of man.

H. But it is as intrinsically feeble as it is morally low. His statement is, "Now, that the individual man is capable of perpetual, or almost perpetual, development, from the day of his birth to the day of his death, is obvious of course." If he had said development, and decay, and extinction (that is, as far as this world goes), he would have been right; but that would not have served his purpose—a cycle of education of the race which ended in decay and extinction is a poor kind of progress. Yet this enters essentially into the condition of man. The sense that he is mortal is a necessary part of his moral existence. A Christian knows it has come in by sin—that it is a silent yet loud-speaking witness of it, and of God's judgment against it. But is the education of the world to end in its progressive death, as well as the rest of its development? If not, the analogy is wholly false, for this is as real and true a part of the course of the individual as his growth from childhood.

W. It is true. I suppose, however, Dr. T. does not consider the world as arrived at its dotage.

H. No; of course all the world were infants or boys till now. Now the human race is left to itself to be guided by the teaching of the *Spirit* within.

W. The human race! Is he a Quaker then?

H. Oh! you must not look for anything like exactitude of thought in drawing-room rationalists. That the mass of men are heathens is all nothing, or that the Bible, of which they profess to be teachers, declares as one of its most solemn truths that the Spirit is given to those who belong to Christ. To speculation, heathenism or Christianity is all alike. It is an element of progress of the human race. You must not be so particular as that. You must believe that the human race is left to itself to be guided by the teaching of the Spirit within.

W. Well, but there is a revelation. Surely Christianity is something. Do they believe that the Son of God is come to seek and save what is lost?

H. Oh! that is part of the progress—one of the things you can sign your assent to as agreeable to the Scriptures, and pass by the side of. It is " humanifying the Divine word."

W. Now do not be bitter. That is not Dr. Temple.

H. It is not; but it is one with whom Dr. Temple, the head master of Rugby, has associated himself, and given his weight to, in the hope that it will be received as an attempt to illustrate the advantage derivable to the cause of religion and moral truth from a free handling, in a becoming spirit, of subjects peculiarly liable to suffer by the repetition of conventional language, and from traditional methods of treatment. You see, however independent of each other, it is a Band of Hope Review. They approve of each other, they consider the Articles as handled in a becoming spirit, though evidently some were a little squeamish in doing it. But we will go on with Dr. Temple.

Man, he tells us, cannot be considered as an individual.

This is a most startling but instructive statement, which I must take up, though I have touched upon it. Note, his soul is individual, his responsibility is individual, his moral state is individual, his feelings are individual, his conscience is individual. All that is elevated, excellent, and that raises him above the common stream of passions, is individual. All that constitutes him a moral being, all the inward man, all in which he is personally related to God, everything that does not perish with his death: and all is ignored, cannot be considered, by Dr. Temple. He is part of a great machine formed by the influences around him, that is all. Neither is he morally individual in himself, according to Dr. Temple; nor raised to be so by a known relationship to God. And this leaks out further on. In speaking of elements of progress, he says, The conviction of the unity and spirituality of God was peculiar to the Jews among the pioneers of civilization. Think of the unity and spirituality of God, or at any rate the conviction of it, making men simply the pioneers of future civilization!

Dr. T. argues that a child, brought up from its birth, apart from its kind, becomes rather a beast in human shape than a man in the full sense at all.

If he used this merely to show that God had so constituted man, that he should learn intelligently from others, and not grow up as animals with a mere instinct, I suppose he needed not have feared much opposition; but when he uses it to show that man cannot be individually considered, it is utterly illogical. That man learns from others does not prove in the least that he is not a responsible individual when he does learn. Dr. Temple's statement destroys totally the whole moral responsibility of man.

That there is progress in knowledge, in civilization, up to a certain point in man's development as a race, is partially true. That a part of the race has been placed under progressive religious light is also true. But that that is the obliteration of individuality, or individual responsibility in and according to that state, is utterly and degradingly false.

If the education at Rugby were necessary to enable a man to go up to Oxford, does that prove he cannot be considered an individual when he is gone up? But all is so carefully generalized as to be false the moment we apply it to facts. Thus Dr. T. says, "We may expect to find in the history of man, each successive age incorporating into itself the substance of the preceding." Now I suppose no intelligent person would deny, that where European civilization has prevailed, the acquirements of one age become, in many points, that is when discoveries are concerned, the elements of the next. Every child who learns astronomy learns the Newtonian, or if you please, the Copernican system, not the Ptolemaic. But when you say the history of man, it is entirely false. The vastly greater part of the human race remain *in statu quo*. The Chinese are not more advanced than they were centuries ago; nor indeed may we say, any of the Asiatic nations, that is, the greatest part by far of the population of the globe. Indeed, they have in many respects retrograded. None of the Africans have advanced; on the contrary there also they have fearfully retrograded. In America, Europeans have supplanted the native population, but there has been no advance save in the conquerors. It is a question if Mexico and Peru are as civilized as when Aztecs and Teczucans possessed the country of Anahuac, and Incas exercised their mild despotism as the legitimate descendants of the sun. There has been a history of man in those races that have come in connection with the despised people of God, but nowhere else. Somehow or other, the people whose records rationalism delights to call in question are the necessary centre, and I may say foundation, of all known history. The mind of man may speculate with interest on other histories, the ruins of Nineveh, and the hundred-gated Thebes ; and Babylon may furnish evidence for antiquaries to build dynasties and histories on ; but a documented history of those early days belongs to Israel only. It may of course be attacked, and conjectures hazarded to disprove it, as they may be hazarded to make kings out of tombs, and centuries out of priestly traditions ; butin Israel alone are the documents there to be disproved. In this history only do we find the principles which Dr. T. speaks of as the true education of man. We will speak afterwards of the influence of Greeks and Romans on the present age and education of man, but they have nothing to do with his analogy of educational epochs, which are, the law, Christ, and the Spirit : for of course we must decently christianize everything, that is, reduce Christianity to the level of man and his progress. And this introduces another immensely important point carefully suppressed by Dr. T. in his account of this progress of man. I mean, the fact of revelation. He speaks of the progress of man ; but the facts in which the progress is estimated are, really, exclusively revelations and interventions of God. He says, " First, the law, then the Son of man, then the gift of the Spirit." Is this progress essential to a spiritual being ? Is this each generation receiving the benefits of the cultivation of that which preceded it ?

But let us consider the facts. However he may borrow the principles of his education of the human race from scripture—except to array himself in these borrowed plumes, revelation is totally ignored and all it contains. If there has been a fall, the progress of the human race, save in its lower aspects, comes to nothing at once. We are fallen beings. There is a guilty soul before God : the whole scene is one departed from and out of the condition

D

He set it in. It is in progress in what, then? It wants, and wants individually, and in every way, restoration— progress in its highest relationship. Christianity, and all the revelation from which the head master of Rugby quotes his principles of progress, treats man as in this state of alienation from God. It is false, or the theory is false. The law was given, but broken. The Son of man in the world, but rejected out of it by man, and a work of redemption revealed for a being not in progress, but lost. I reserve the consideration of what thoughts that man must have of God, who, looking at this world's universal state, does not believe in the fall of man.

But further, as to the world's history. The flood has taken place : so the Old Testament teaches, so the Lord declares ; as Peter warns that it is by wilful ignorance it is forgotten. But if the flood has taken place, the whole race has been judged once, and judged for the progress it had made. That judgment will, it is true, not be repeated, but the now world is reserved for fire. At what point of progress will that come? Has Dr. T. ever heard of days in which mockers will be, who say, Where is the pro- mise of His coming? for all things continue as they were —of perilous times that will come, in which the scriptures will be the resource of the faithful who continue in the things they have learned?

But I am wrong to reason on scripture with them, as if they believed it. Let us take their own system as they take it up professedly from scripture. That I am not unjust in charging them with ignoring this mighty dealing of God with the world, which, while keeping the place they do, they have not the honest boldness to deny, while intro- ducing what sets it aside, you may easily see. Dr. T.'s words are these : "The education of this early race may strictly be said to begin when it was formed into the various masses out of which the nations of the earth have sprung. The world, as it were, went to school, and was broken up into classes." Now that refers to the confusion of tongues at Babel. You would suppose that, before this Rugby education of the race, when a wise master began to deal with and educate it, in order that there might be some hope of the race's turning out well, it had been as yet nurtured in the graceful affections and first confiding impressions of the home of its childhood. Alas! no. It was a world outcast from God—so bad that He had to destroy it. The childhood of man, before it went to school, according to Dr. T., was violence, and that followed by sensuality, fallen or not. But the flood—no trace of it is found.

We are told, that the earliest commands almost entirely refer to bodily appetites and sensual passions. This may suit the theory, because they have to be corrected as children, but is otherwise a dream. There is no command before the flood, and after it the one declaration is, " Whoso sheddeth man's blood, by man shall his blood be shed." It appears that wilfulness of temper, germs of wanton cruelty, characterize childhood, and are easily corrected by a mother; but here there was no education, no wise educator. The Governor of the world left the childhood of man to itself, to run into wanton violence unrestrained, to perfect its evil education without any restraint at all. This was a singular system of the education of the human race. " Each generation receiving the benefit of the cultivation of that which precedes it." " The easily corrected cruelty was here," we are told, " developed into a prevailing plague of wickedness."

Now let the reader remember that this was, to take

Hebrew dates, as long a period nearly as since Christ—some sixteen hundred and fifty-six years; but this is not all; from thence to the giving of the law there were some eight hundred years. That is, during some two thousand five hundred years the race did not get any education at all; and, if that history is to be believed which Dr. Temple *uses as his proof* of the value of the education, the whole race, save eight persons, had been destroyed because of the result of the education they had given themselves. But this is not only a discrepancy in the analogy, but it upsets the whole system. There was no such education going on. The world went on on another principle; leaving man, not without witness indeed from God, but otherwise to himself and with no education. And, if scripture is to be believed as to one of the most solemnly attested facts in it, the whole world was judged once, before its alleged *education began.*

But here we stumble on another strange instance of the falseness of all this. I quote still Dr. Temple. " The world was once a child under tutors and governors, until the time appointed by the Father. . . . The education of the world, like that of the child, begins with the law." Now, note, not only was there two thousand five hundred years of the race without any education at all, if we pass over the flood, and the whole world judged if there was, and the theory an absurdity; but, even supposing this left aside, the facts are misstated. " The education," Dr. T. tells us, " of this early race may strictly be said to begin when it was formed into the various masses out of which the nations of the earth have sprung." That was at Babel, or in Peleg's time; but there were some seven hundred years between Peleg and the law, so that the education of the human race began seven hundred years before it began. And I pray you to remark, that this is not a question of confounding chronology with a great principle. The theory of Dr. Temple is, that the dividing into nations strictly begins the education; it was the forming them into classes. But the very vital principle of his system of analogy with individual education is, that it began with law, but there were more than seven centuries between the two. I suppose the classes at Rugby are in before Dr. Temple. That we may admit. At least they used to be as a rule, at Westminster, when I was there; but if Dr. Temple were to leave some period analogical to seven centuries before he came, I am afraid the sanction of the law, not the law, would be wanting. What riot in the schoolroom! It is true, the present generation may have profited by the cultivation of the last; but at any rate, in my time we should have had notable confusion. But we will be serious. Dr. Temple will forgive my recollections of these early days; he tells us they are often vividly remembered. But I turn to our scripture history; and you will see the whole principle of the theory proved false.

Scripture treats man as a sinner to be restored to God or judged: rationalists, as a race to be educated, and the previous parts sacrificed to the condition of a little fragment at the end. It is a base idea, but it is its justness we have now to think of. Now in scripture we are carefully told that, in the sense in which there was an education and progress in it, law was not the beginning. The promise came four hundred and thirty years before it. Now this is an all-important principle. It brings in God, whom Dr. Temple leaves out. Grace, only in germ it is true, precedes law, and law comes in by the bye as a needed convincer of the conscience. That is the Divine, the blessed form of education revealed in the word, because it reveals God, and must reveal, therefore, love and grace. Law may be needed. It was needed. The question of righteousness must be raised. But God had to say to it, and grace and goodness and love must be the point of departure with Him, because He is it, and is it with man. Dr. Temple's is an education of man without God; and therefore, as he cannot deny " the prevailing plague of wickedness," he begins with man's only remedy, commandments, to an unintelligent nature. But think of such a scheme which lets the person to be educated get to a prevailing plague of wickedness before he begins to educate him! It is well Dr. T. leaves God out.

But this confusion of Peleg's time and the law, this lapse of some seven centuries, omits facts which show in another respect the falseness of the whole system. After Babel or Peleg's time, when nationalities and races had been formed, a kind of departure from God came in of which we find no trace before. Not violence and evil; that is the recorded state of man before the flood. Now, man had been forced to recognise divine judgments. But, far from the true God, yea, not liking to retain the true God in his knowledge, he changed the truth of God into a lie, and worshipped and served the creature more than the Creator—changed the glory of the incorruptible God into an image made like unto corruptible man, and to birds, and four-footed beasts, and creeping things. Your fathers, says Joshua, worshipped other gods beyond the flood (Terah, the father of Abraham, and the father of Nahor). Now the God of glory appears to Abraham, and calls him to leave entirely the system into which, as Dr. Temple justly remarks, God had formed the world—countries, and kindreds, and father's house. The world was broken up into classes; but when God began to educate, He called out of all the classes one to be for Himself; not indeed by law, but then He gave the promises. The principle of a called people, or saint, was brought out, and Abraham became, as an immense principle, the father of the faithful, who were known as called out of the world. That the world was educated by it is absolutely false. The world, or the nations, had rejected God altogether, and taken devils to be their gods; and God, patient in mercy, begins a race of His own, calls Abraham and his seed, be they in the flesh or in the Spirit.

I have partially noticed some particular proofs of the progress of the world according to Dr. Temple and his companions; but, as they belong to this epoch, I will refer to one or two of their discoveries here. Lamech makes no comparison of himself with God whatever: it is all a dream, unless taking vengeance is comparing one-self with God, because vengeance belongs to Him. If so, many are guilty of it still, I fear. At any rate, he compares himself with Cain, and he is not God, I suppose. As to the gross ignorance about building a tower high enough to escape God's wrath, it is, without any contempt of Dr. Temple, his ignorance, not that of the sons of Noah. They acted very wisely according to man. They made (what Nebuchadnezzar tried afterwards, and a man who founds empires ever does) a great public centre which could be a name—which God alone ought to have or give—that they might not be scattered, but have united force. It was to be a Rome in the world. It was not ignorance, but profound political skill; but it met the power of one who had other purposes, and under His hand it brought on the very thing they wished to avoid. They built a city and a tower, a central capital to unite them all as one great company, and a tower which should distinguish itself, and to which all should be bound as belonging to it. Dr. Temple's notion is ignorance of the nineteenth century after, not of the twenty-second before, Christ.

But to return to our history. God separates a people carefully from the world, and gives them a law when He has separated them. The world was never under tutors and governors at all. When God dealt with the world, He returned, and returned necessarily, to the principle of grace, on which alone, even if law existed, He could really deal with the sinner. The education of the world never began with law. The world never had any law. God did give a law to a carefully isolated people, and carefully isolated them by it; made, as it is expressed, a middle wall of partition, so that if a Jew associated himself with the world, he was a defiled and guilty Jew. No doubt in this law great principles of moral government lay (I may almost say) concealed; but this only proves still more the great truth. God must separate a people out of the world to deposit, in a system carefully excluding others, the perfect rule of creature estate; and to preserve the knowledge of one true God in a world given to idols in their will, and given up by Him to a reprobate mind to work all uncleanness with greediness (as every one who has studied the working of heathen idolatry knows they were, and indeed are; and the whole system to be a consecration of vice in its filthiest and most abhorrent shapes). Yet these efforts of God with Israel were fruitless, and the law given in vain. Israel first went after idols; and when that unclean spirit was gone out, their house was empty, swept, and garnished. They neglected the pearl which the blessed Lord drew out of the setting of the law, turned its outward ceremonies,

which unregenerate flesh could perform, into their righteousness, and hardened themselves against grace and Him
that brought it.

So true is it that the law was not given to the world to
educate it, and the education of the world is not in God's
thought, that Israel, in order to be taken as a people, is
redeemed out of it. Till that redemption there is no
dwelling of God with man—not in paradise, not with
Abraham. When redemption is even figuratively presented,
it is said (Exod. xxix.), "I have brought them out of the
land of Egypt that I may dwell among them." Hence,
as God's dwelling with man is never seen, so holiness is
never spoken of till then. Because redemption is necessary
to man's being near God, and that is (morally understood)
holiness. The moment (Exod. xv.) Israel is out of Egypt,
holiness is spoken of. No doubt, all this was in an outward carnal way then; but the principle taught is all-
important. Doubtless there were holy persons before;
but here great principles are revealed.

W. Well, I must say that this effect is produced on my
mind by the facts you have gone through: If we are to
take the scripture account of facts—(and what you have
remarked is true that, save ignoring the flood, Dr. Temple's statements, are based on scripture statements)
but if we are to take them—not only is he mistaken
as to the alleged facts, but (what is far more important)
if the Scripture view be true, his is totally false. It
is not a question of details of ancient history which a
rationalist might contest, but the whole principle on
which God has dealt with man is the opposite of that on
which Dr. Temple estimates what has taken place. It
seems to me very shallow indeed. It shelters itself under
references to Scripture, which might seem to give credit

to the statements with those who have not yet thrown off
all respect for those wonderful records; but when examined, it has not a shadow of foundation. The Bible
is false in its own teaching, or Dr. Temple's views are as
unfounded as they are trifling and superficial. I am glad
of this conversation : for, though I rejected the principles
of the book as really infidel, and morally unsatisfactory,
I had not an idea of the hollowness of its views, at least
thus far. The utter want of honesty of the part which
speaks of consenting and allowing had offended me, as
contrary to all uprightness. I confess that turned me at
once away from all confidence. I cannot conceive how a
man could openly avow such principles. But I had not
examined the reasonings.

H. Mark another thing, dear W. It is a point to me
most striking in the character of this system. You may
have the law for a schoolmaster, Christ and the primitive
Church for an example, the Spirit to set you free and
leave you to yourself to be guided by the Spirit within ;
you may have Greece to teach you taste, cultivation, and
logic; Rome self-restraint, obedience, and patriotism;
mediæval popery to keep Clovis in order : but God revealing Himself, revealing Himself in love, so as to draw
out the heart, to teach it goodness by its enjoying it, so as
to link the heart with Himself, and raise it above carnal
and worldly and selfish interests of this low and sin-
ridden world—God producing the reflection of His own
nature in the thankful and enlightened heart—God
revealing Himself to man, so that he should taste and
enjoy what He is—no, that must not be; the thought of
being thus imitators of God as dear children—you must
not seek it here. Everything but God, everything for
man to think well of himself by, to be what Paul calls

gain to him, that is, the nurture of self; but God—no : no revelation of Him must enter into the education of man.

W. It is true. This is immensely important. How often one reads books without seeing what is underneath the surface! But this is indeed grave; the whole moral education of man, without his being brought into heart-association with God by the elevating revelation of Him. I see it is anti-christian in principle, anti-divine. It lowers the whole of what is carrying on in man to what he is in flesh, and thus separates from God, instead of bringing to Him in living capacity to enjoy Him, and making man morally like Him. I have difficulty (do you know) in expressing what the effect is on my mind: for leaving God out makes all so false, that it is impossible to express anything then fully. A being who can exist truly only in relation to another can have no truth of his existence without introducing the other.

H. To be sure; and then if he be a sinner, introducing that other must be accompanied by that which reconciles the sinner to that nature according to its own holy and blessed qualities. This brings in redemption; and the education of the world is trifling, immoral nonsense You must give up that which alone elevates man, his association with God, or associate him with Him according to what He is. The nature and character of God must be maintained, or it is not with *Him* I am associated. And I must have morally the qualities which judge of good and evil as He does to be really associated with Him. But I do judge the evil, and see the guilt. Now Christianity meets this, and gives me a full blessing, because it gives me life. "He that hath the Son hath life." He is a life-giving Spirit. But then, besides that, it takes away all guilt from me. I can judge evil fully in my heart and conscience, because I know I shall never be judged for it—that Christ has *by Himself* purged my sins, and sat down on the right hand of the Majesty on high. I affirm that without these two principles, a new life, and the perfect purging of sins according to God's nature by redemption, no real moral elevation of man can take place; because he cannot be spiritually associated with God according to the perfection of God's nature. The communication of the Divine nature, though absolutely necessary, does not suffice, because the communication of that nature makes one judge evil as God does, at any rate in principle. I see the selfishness and impurity that is in man's mind—that is now in mine; and, *for that very reason*, I see guilt and wretchedness in myself; I have the conscience of evil or guilt (not necessarily by crimes or vices, but by comparing my whole inward life with the loveliness of the Divine nature) on my soul; my conscience must be purged for God, as a consciously responsible creature before Him, that my heart may be free before Him, that His holy nature, which must repel evil, and which is the very source of my delight, may be maintained even for my soul to enjoy.

W. I see this very plainly—what God is must be morally maintained for my soul, if I am to enjoy Him. If it is, I must judge sin as He does (that is, if I am honest myself). It is a gain, in a certain sense, to have a bad conscience in this way.

H. Yes; but a terrible burden, because sin separates from God, though we see He is love. But the purging the conscience by a work done without us, and which is perfect in glorifying God, gives me an unhindered delight in Him, and, I may add, in the love which has done it. God has put this in the simplest way (blessed be His name!) for simple souls, but it is of the deepest moral necessary truth. You may have amiable men, but no God if you have not this. When reading a work of Maurice's (a person of whom I know nothing, and speak, of course, only of his works)—

W. You mean him who wrote a work on Sacrifice, and Essays. I should like to know what you think of him.

H. I speak only of his books, I repeat, for I know nothing of him. I should say he was an amiable man, with many elements of a fine nature, though with amazing confidence in himself—a trait which sometimes accompanies a fine benevolent nature, when it is not humbled in a Christian way by the knowledge of itself and the supreme excellence of God and what we are—our wretched, selfish, approbation-loving hearts. I should think, too, his books show wants, perhaps divinely given wants, in the soul; but I should think the influences his soul had been under were half Socinian and half Quaker. But he has no knowledge at all of the effect of having a conscience before God. I said all along as I read (I forget which of his books), This man does not believe in guilt; and when I had got on a very considerable way in the book (two hundred or three hundred pages, I should think), I found " guilt, that is, guile." * Now there you can get the key to his whole story. He may have judged some evil, but he has never had his conscience before God at all. Hence he can turn what that gives into a play on words, or a question of etymology; but what a

* I apprehend this is a mere blunder. Guile is the same as wile; and guilt, a Saxon word, fine or punishment (as now, in German, " vergelten ").

tale that tells! Ah! what a difference it makes when a soul has to say to God.

W. I see plainly now both what was attractive in his views and the mischievous tendency they had, the mischievous influence they exercised on my soul. In fact, it strikes at the *responsibility* of man, our relationship to God.

H. To be sure it does. Holiness is the quality of a nature which repels evil in its nature, and delights in what is good. Righteousness is founded really on the same principle, but brings in the authority of God, which judges of this and the responsibility of the creature. Now man will admit holiness, because that exalts man, makes him like God, excellent in himself—he has " no guile;" righteousness he does not, because this asserts God's authority—the creature's responsibility. It is making good God's authority against evil by judgment—our real relationship to God. This man will not submit to. He is willing to be free from guile : it exalts him in his own sight. But to be under guilt—no: that humbles him.

W. How subtle evil is!

H. Yes; but a personal conscience makes all simple. I do not discuss with a bad conscience; I can principles with my reason. With a bad conscience I want cleansing, and, because I have offended a loving Father and God, forgiveness too; and, thank God, I have it in Christ. There is no personal having to do with God without this. I may theorize, and honestly enjoy my ideas; but theorizing is not the knowledge of God. A truly upright soul, a divinely taught soul, has a moral need that the love of God, the favour which is its light and its joy, should be a righteous favour (as scripture speaks, Grace reigns through righteousness)—hence, that God should righteously not see sin upon it; it has need, therefore, that the conscience should be purged. And this it has through the truth, that the blood of Jesus Christ, His Son, cleanses from all sin. Without it, God's love would be an unholy love—would not be God or love at all. We walk in the *light*, as God is in the light; and the blood of Jesus Christ, His Son, cleanses us from all sin. Hence comes that bright and blessed testimony, though there in outward figures, " He hath not seen iniquity in Jacob, nor beheld perverseness in Israel."

W. I confess I see no moral perfection maintainable without this (for sin there is in the world), no true assurance of heart with God, no uprightness in man. And association with God, fellowship, is the one true and excellent blessing that belongs to us in this world, and the next.

H. Surely. But we will pursue our essay, though I have not, I believe, much more to say.

The principle of the essay is, each successive age incorporating into itself the substance of the preceding. The analogy is, the law, Christ, and the Spirit. But this wholly contradicts the principle. These are no incorporations of past growth or acquirements, but specific revelations of a full and absolute character in themselves —indeed, as to the last two, the actual coming of divine persons. Not only so, but the law was given when men had plunged into every loathsome wickedness, and had learnt to worship devils instead of God; so that God had given them up to a reprobate mind, even as to what became them as men. And it was given therefore to a people carefully separated from the rest of the world.

It was no progress; it was a revelation to a peculiar people. When Christ came, it was after this had been broken, and the people become a whited sepulchre. He likewise, though introducing universal principles, separates a people to Himself, and is entirely rejected by men. When the Holy Ghost comes, we know, on the Lord's own authority, that the world cannot receive Him, "because it seeth Him not, neither knoweth Him."

In a word, it was no progressive incorporation by one age of the acquirements of the last; but revelations given to a people separated to receive them. The first, because men had departed utterly from God; the second, because the depositaries of the first had broken and falsified it, as they crucified Him who came. As to the third, it was manifested in power at the first; and instead of progress or development, there has been a corruption by the denial of the presence of the Spirit, and setting aside the word, which has made the annals of the Church the most painful history the world can show (as has been insultingly said, the annals of hell); and if the degradation of heathenism was more open, it was not so morally abominable, nor clothed with the forms of Christian grace. Sin among heathens was horrible to the last degree, and consecrated to deities who were only devils to help men's lusts; but there were no Christian indulgences to allow or forgive it; no tax for what it was to be compounded at; no selling of grace and licence for what was condemned. This was reserved for what is called the Church (and in the outward sense justly).

And remark here another point of vast importance in the present day when development is so much spoken of. What God reveals is revealed perfect in its place and for its purpose at first; and man declines from it. There is

progress in the character of God's revelations, compared
with one another; but in themselves, none. There cannot
be progress in a revelation. It is itself. There may be
in revelations. A revelation is given perfect. Man
declines from it or corrupts it. That man should make
progress in a revelation denies its nature. Now the
things Dr. Temple speaks of were revelations—different
in nature, but still revelations. And when I come to
Christ, I find another immensely important truth—to talk
of progress here is blasphemy. He is God manifest in
flesh. He is perfection. Hence the apostle John tells
us to abide in that which we have heard from the
beginning.

And I find here too a principle of Scripture, the ignorance and denial of which is the root of all these errors
and modern reasonings. The Scripture (I am not now to
enquire whether *its whole system* be false) presents Christ
as a *second* man, a new starting point of the human race,
the last Adam. There is no progress of man in flesh
spoken of : he is to put off the old man, or has done so,
and put on the new, which after God is created in righteousness and true holiness. He is to reckon himself dead; he
is crucified with Christ. He speaks of when we *were* in
the flesh. That is, the blessed and admirable doctrine of
Scripture is the absolute moral judgment of man as man,
a child of Adam in flesh, because sin is there; and,
through the delight the new man has in God, he cannot
bear this. He has crucified the flesh with the affections
and lusts, and lives as alive to God in the last man. "I
am crucified with Christ; nevertheless, I live : yet not I,
but Christ liveth in me."

And the great ordinances of Christianity declare this as
its nature. We are buried in baptism unto death, risen

E

again, and we celebrate a Christ in the Lord's Supper, not who has instructed us (though blessedly He has done so those who are quickened, and warned the dead) but died for us. Thus Christianity is founded on the total condemnation of the old man (only that Christ has died for it in grace, and thus as a sacrifice for sin condemned sin in the flesh), and the introduction of a new, but a new connected in the power of Christ's resurrection with that which is heavenly, where Christ now sits. The object of this new life is not here, though its display is. It is the true character of power in a creature to live in the circumstances it is in, from motives and a power which are not found in them, or else he is governed by them (that is, is weak). So with the Christian, with peace in his conscience through a dying Christ, he has a heavenly Christ before him, and, his motives being wholly out of this world, he has, through grace, power to live in it according to the character of the motives which govern him.

This is not the place to unfold all the exquisite internal beauty of this principle, wrought out for its perfecting in dependence on grace, in the midst of the conflicts in which we are in a world of evil, with a lower nature in itself prone to it; and the continual association with Christ, our glorified Head, the Man at God's right hand, in which it is made good, so as to grow up to Him who is the Head in all things. This would be to unfold the contents of all the epistles as the development of it in teaching, and the gospels as the exhibition of the perfection of it in Christ: but I have said enough to show that the system of the New Testament is the setting aside of the old man, the flesh, the first Adam, because there is sin (and sin is become unbearable when the true light, Christ, is in the heart as life), and the possession, the substitution for that, of the new man, Christ our life, unfolded in a life which we live by the faith of the Son of God, who loved us, and gave Himself for us. Was He a point of progress in the development of human nature or Adam fallen life? or the perfect exhibition of a new thing—that eternal life which was with the Father, and was manifested to us, and became the source of it to others, while He has died for the guilt and sin which characterized the old?

W. I see it is indeed an immensely important principle. It strikes at the root of all this system. This builds up what Scripture calls the old man, and develops it. You say, its principle in fallen man is sin and self, and that God has in Christ introduced a new life in Christ, and to others through Him; and as He has cleansed from sin, so He has given a heavenly object out of this world. But then do you mean that no one had this life till Christ came down to earth?

H. No, of course not. Life and incorruptibility were brought to light by the gospel; but this life did not begin to exist then. Christ, who is the Lord from heaven, is a life-giving Spirit—has not merely a living soul, though that He had of course : and He communicated this life to others, from Abel, I may well say and doubt it not, from Adam downwards. But then, for that very reason, though the great contrast, the enmity of man—of the carnal mind —against God was not brought out till the cross, when the perfection of God revealed in flesh was fully presented, those who partook of this life through grace were hated and rejected of the world, whose boasted progress is depicted to us by the new philosophy. " He that was born after the flesh persecuted him that was born after the Spirit." They were moral contradictions : one loved God,

judged self, and owned God's authority; the other sought
self, and would none of God for that reason. Conscience
there was and is in all; conscience judges good and evil:
but a new life is good in a Divine way. Hence you will
find that, with all this modern school of rationalism, even
in its most infidel forms, Christ will be recognised, provided He be a restorer of what the Scripture denounces as
flesh. They will use what appears Christian language to
many a simple mind. But the just condemnation of a
sinner, the absolute condemnation of flesh, and a new life
in Christ, and atonement for the sin of the old—all this
will not be heard of; and into the antichristian system
even Christians fall. It exalts man; and all the blessed
light of God, the heavenly place into which Christ is
entered, is lost.

W. But what do you say to the other elements of
human progress, Egypt, Greece, Rome, and the like?

H. If you mean civilization, arts, and mental development, and cultivation, and more particularly science, I do
not of course deny it; though I think there is a good
deal of mistake as to it. Discoveries, by which the knowledge of nature or the power of man over it is advanced,
are undoubtedly multiplied. We know more physical
facts than our ancestors. Astronomy, geology, on the one
hand, and railroads, telegraphs, chemistry, on the other
hand, have enlarged, not the domain, but the appropri-
ation of the domain, allotted to man. And with every
increase of knowledge there is a reaction. There is more
reality and less hypothesis on all these subjects; but I
doubt the development of much more than materialism by
it. That this is a progress I more than doubt. As regards taste and cultivation, or intellectual powers, I should
think also progress more than doubtful. All now is at best

imitation. Take Grecian architecture or Gothic styles (whose ideal conceptions are the opposite one of another), or even Italian, all attempted is imitative. In intellectual power, I suppose Grecian or Roman was as developed in itself as any now. Plato, Aristotle, or what was more profound than either, the British triads or Bardic philosophy,* present the expression of as powerful thought. And as to language, it is admitted that, as an instrument of thought, the Greek stands, of all commonly known languages, unrivalled. The powers of Sanscrit I am unacquainted with, and but little with the capacities of the daughter which most resembles it, they say, the Irish. In philosophy there is more truth in modern times, so far (not, as there has been progress, but) as revelation has exercised an influence on it, and no farther. So that I do not see great progress even in these earthly things. As to philosophy, all is necessarily false at all times, because it reasons upon the present state of man as a normal one, or else it becomes theology, and thereupon, as its necessary point of departure, upon his relationship to God, and what God is. Hence it is all necessarily false, both as to God, and as to man. It is in vain to say that you must not bring your religion into philosophy, because, unless religion be fable, it is the truth, so that it is only saying that you must not bring in truth. There I believe, they have told the truth. That man is not fallen is a calumny against God. A God who made this world directly as it is, would be a weak or a cruel God. But if man be fallen and in rebellion, and have to say to God in that state; if his whole moral condition be the acquired knowledge of good and evil, far from the source

* But here the influence of Christianity is evident, as in Neoplatonism.

of good, then reasoning upon his relationships to God to prove what they are normally is to reason always against the truth. And that goes far deeper into the whole system than men are generally aware of. It affects every possible relationship of life. It is the reason there are magistrates, the origin of property, of labour, death, inheritances. I take the commonest, every-day, outward things on purpose. Philosophy, since it ceased to be cosmogony, is reasoning on morality, ignorant of the groundwork of the highest obligations, and of the whole state of things on which moral relationships are founded. Nothing can be right or set right, if the world has departed from God (because all its state is wrong—the central obligation is, which was the groundwork of all others, though those others be true) unless we bring in the restoring power of *revealed* goodness applied to that state, and this is Christianity. Hence it is a necessary consequence, that all philosophy is and must be, false. There is evidence enough that evil exists. The man who will say that things are morally as they ought to be is a devil, and not a man, take heathens or Christendom. If they are not, there is no sense in not beginning with the truth of this state and its remedy, if there be one. But this is religious truth.

W. But you have made a sweeping clearance of philosophy.

H. Truth always does. The mind may be interested in it as an exercise; my own has been, though I never pursued it far. Truth, as to its title at least, had too early possession of my mind. But you cannot deny that speculation, whose starting-point is false, can but plunge the mind farther in error the farther it goes. There is no ποῦ στῶ. It is far worse than the play of Hamlet with the part of Hamlet left out. That to which all refers is wanting. If I leave out God, all is essentially false; and if I bring Him in, and omit the groundwork of *all* present relationship with man as he really is (that is, a state of sin), all must be equally false. Sin is the groundwork of all God's dealings now.

W. Dear! How do you mean that? That is a strange statement, is it not?

H. Is not judgment in respect of sin?

W. Well, of course it is.

H. So much so that there could be none without it—hence *in itself* can only be condemnation. If God judges His own workmanship as it came out of His hands, He is judging Himself, not the work, or, if you please, in the work. But if it has departed wilfully into rebellion, judgment as such must be condemnation.

W. But if man had never fallen, would there not have been a judgment?

H. A judgment of what?

W. Well, I do not know.

H. Nor can you know. There was nothing to judge, speaking of human nature: all was then as God made it. If man has abandoned God and gone into sin, I repeat, judgment must be condemnation; and that is the ground Christianity goes upon. Christ comes to seek and to save the lost. And so every Divinely taught soul: "Enter not into judgment with thy servant, O Lord; for in thy sight shall no man living be justified." But I pursue my theme a little. Is not the exercise of mercy in respect of sin?

W. Of course.

H. And law?

W. Why yes, law forbids it.

H. And grace?

W. Of course.

H. And salvation, and judgments, and patience, or vengeance—all is in respect of sin. Hence, the immensely deep moral development in the soul in its relationship with God. No angel would know God, or be in the kind of relationship in which a sinner brought to God is. All the highest attributes and qualities in the Godhead are brought out—mercy, patience, goodness, condescension, love in its perfect exercise in the shape of grace, on one side, and restoring in righteousness on the other to perfect delight in itself, in a word, redemption. The intimacy which the working of grace, whether in the incarnation or in the soul of one in whom grace is, the estimate of good and evil, by the proximity of what is Divine to evil as it is in us; yea, the communication of what is Divine to one who, on the other side, is weakness, and yet wilfulness and self, the dependence of a creature who has both on continual grace, and yet the capacity of the enjoyment of the highest good—all this, which is not Christianity exactly, but its working in us, gives a display of Divine wisdom, a purifying and elevating process, a knowledge of God in His highest nature, most intimate, and yet most adoring, which makes philosophy puny and dry beyond all belief, empty, utterly empty. Christianity is light and love come into darkness and selfishness, and in the human heart reaching all its springs, and destroying self, by showing it and replacing it by God; and this, not by the flimsy spinnings of the human brain, but by a Divine person; who, if Divine desires are wrought in me, takes me out of myself by Divine affections, instead of exalting self, by producing in it qualities to be admired, which being by self makes them bad and false. The Christian, *quâ*

Christian, has Divine qualities, but sees, and because he sees, only God.

W. Why you are growing quite eloquent! But it is true.

H. There is nothing so eloquent as Christianity itself. Did you never remark, that Christianity makes the poorest mind eloquent? What is eloquence? Is it not elevated thoughts, clothed in what is perfectly adapted to the meanest capacity, and enjoyed because it lifts the poor heart, wearied with common-place life and toil, out of itself? Now, this is what Christianity does, because it reveals a Divine person, God Himself, who has adapted Himself to the lowest, yea, the vilest; who is holy enough (for He is perfect in it) to bring love into all the recesses of the human heart, because never defiled Himself, and awake, even by its sorrows and its miseries, the want of, and to the enjoyment of, the love that has visited it. It has set too, by a glorious redemption and atonement, the poor soul, that by love has learned to delight in light, at liberty to enjoy it, because it is spotless in it, and the adoring object of the love that has brought it there.

I look around. What can I see? Heathenism, men worshipping stocks and stones; Christendom, what would often disgrace a heathen; yet goodness and wisdom evidenced in the midst of it all. What can I think? All is confusion. The goodness and wisdom I see lead me in spite of me to God, and the thoughts of God confound me when I see all the evil; philosophy, poor philosophy, would justify evil to justify God. But when I see Christ, the riddle is gone. I see perfect good in the midst of the evil, occupied with it, and then suffering under it. My heart rests. I find one object that satisfies all its wants—rises above all its cravings. I have what is good in goodness itself. I see what is above evil which was pressing on me. My heart has got rest in good, and a good which is such in the midst of and above evil, and that is what I want; and I have got relief, because I have found in that One what is power over it.

But I go a little farther, and I get a great deal more. I follow this blessed One, from whom all have received good, and who has wrought it with unwearied patience, and I hear the shouts of a giddy multitude, and I trace the dark plans of jealous enemies—man who cannot bear good; I see high judges who cannot occupy themselves with what is despised in the world, and would quiet malice by letting it have its way, and goodness the victim of it. But a little thought leads me to see in a nearer view what man is—hatred against God and good. Oh! what a display! The truest friend denies, the nearest betrays, the weaker ones who are honest flee; priests, set to have compassion on ignorant failure, plead furiously against innocence; the judge washing his hands of condemned innocence; goodness absolutely alone, and the world—all men—enmity, universal enmity, against it. Perfect light has brought out the darkness; perfect love, jealous hatred. Self would have its way and not have God, and the cross closes the scene as far as man is concerned. The carnal mind is enmity against God.

But oh! here is what I want. Oh! where can I turn from myself? Can I set up to be better than my neighbours? No, it is myself. The sight of a rejected Christ has discovered myself to myself, the deepest recesses of my heart are laid bare, and self, horrible self, is there. But not on the cross: there is none. And the infinite love of God rises and shines in its own perfection above it all. I can adore God in love, if I abhor myself. Man is met, risen above, set aside in his evil, absolute as it is in itself when searched out. The revelation of God in Christ has proved it in all its extent on the cross. That was hatred against love in God; but it was perfect love to those that were hating it, and love when and where they were such. It was the perfect hatred of man, and the perfect love of God doing for him that hated Him, what put away the hatred and blotted out the sin that expressed it. There is nothing like the cross. It is the meeting of the perfect sin of man with the perfect love of God—sin risen up to its highest point of evil and gone, put away, and lost in its own worst act. God is above man even in the height of his sin; not in allowing it, but in putting it away by Christ dying for it in love. The soldier's insulting spear, the witness if not the instrument of death, was answered by the blood and water which expiated and purified from the blow which brought it out. Sin was known, and, to have a true heart, it must be known, and God was known—known in light, and the upright heart wants that, but known in perfect love, before which we had no need to hide or screen the sin; no sin allowed, but no sin left on the conscience. All our intercourse with God founded on this—grace reigning through righteousness. Shall we turn to learn of Greeks and Romans after this?

W. God forbid! It is a wonderful scene. There is, in truth, nothing like it.

H. Nothing in heaven or earth, save He who was there for us. The glory we shall share with Him; but on the cross He was alone. He remains alone in its glory. Associated with Him there nothing can be, save as it is the expression of the nature which was revealed and glorified in it. That we find ever in God who is thus known. Eternal life is become thus association with God.

But, though reluctantly, I must turn again to our essay, to the effort to supplant the cross, for such it is, by the progress of corrupt human nature—the cross, which writes death on corrupt man, and brings in a new and Divine man risen up out of that death, and a walk in newness of life. The system, however, we have discussed, as far as a brief conversation will allow; but there are two or three passages which it may be useful to notice, some of them showing the animus of this and of all these essays, and of the whole school, and the miserable ground on which they stand.

As to mere intellectual progress in the sphere of knowledge, no one, of course, questions it. I may pass over Egypt, though boasted Greece was, as the Egyptian priests told Herodotus, a shallow copy turned into poetry of far deeper moral intuitions found in Egyptian mythology—deeper, because nearer the source of ancient truths. But as to Greece and Rome, no one denies that, as regards the upper orders, they exercise an influence over the minds of the present age in virtue of their education. Whether it be in all respects an advantage may be doubted. They are not what is highest in motive or thought, I judge; but so it is. That there is progress, I cannot exactly see in it, because we *go back* for models and influence. If Rome had been forgotten, and we were a fuller and riper development of what was gone by, I should understand progress. But this is not so. We try and get back to what they displayed. How that is progress, I do not understand. In progress I leave behind what preceded me. Copying Raphael (if I can) is

not progress in painting beyond Raphael, though that
copying exercise an influence over me.   Then as to
patriotism; it is human nature.   Εἰς αἰωνὸς ἄριστος
ἀμύνεσθαι περὶ πάτρης was before Rome was heard of.   If
we desire to learn how consummate selfishness, which
broke through every honourable and generous feeling,
and trampled on all the world, disguised itself under the
name of patriotism, we may surely learn it in Rome; and
how democracy or human will closed in servility, and
tried to hide its pain when oppressed in letting loose the
same will in vice, we may go to Rome.   If Greece have
given reason and taste, I can only repeat, this is not
progress in us.   If heartlessness and poetry for conscience, if vanity and talent are a model, Greece may
shine pre-eminent.   Cultivation I admit, as far as it can
go on without morality.   But immoral beauty, and such
was the mind of Greece, which excludes the truly Divine
(for even Plato declared the impossibility of any direct
connection between the supreme God and a creature,
whence probably Justin Martyr did too), which has the
creatures of imagination, not of spiritual need for gods,
which does not look at another world—such beauty as
this, admitting in the fullest way its very high development there, is a very doubtful subject of admiration,
however it may call out certain faculties, which no one
denies.   A lively imagination connected with excessive
vanity, and identified with immorality, is not a picture
which attracts me.   "What sort of morality the Gentiles
would have handed down to us .   .   . ," Dr. Temple
tells us, "is clear."   I do not know (though the destruction of mental purity is a great evil) whether, with the
present attempt to exalt human nature, it might not be
well that maturer minds, at any rate, should know the

excessive, atrocious, disgusting immorality of all classical, and indeed all heathen iniquity, the universal depravity, besides what is discovered by mythological and historical research. It might be painful to such minds, and they abhorrent from it; but it would act as a warning and preventive against such views as those of the "Essays and Reviews." It has been said, and said truly, that no decent persons would allow on their tables in English what is learnt by all classically educated youths at school. I may be told they do not rest on it—be it so; but they become familiar with it in what they are taught to admire. Any one may see the picture of vaunted antiquity in Romans i. That, Dr. Temple tells us, is what is to teach the world; ay, the Christian world too. There is beauty, there is patriotism. What do I learn from this? That these passions of human nature and elements of his being are perfectly compatible with the most degraded possible state in which human nature can be found. Nothing could possibly exceed the degradation, by vices which eat out everything naturally noble even in nature, in which these Greeks and Romans lived. The beauty and the patriotism amused or absorbed them so that they should not find it out. Stifled conscience needed folly or pride.

W. But it is difficult to know what to do. Are we to leave young men uncultivated?

H. Difficulties there must be in a world in which sin has made deadly confusion. But there comes in the noble active principle of Christianity: "To him that over-cometh;" "Be of good cheer, I have overcome the world." Christianity gives motives, objects, energies, which deliver man, when under their influence, from slavery to the scene through which he is passing. He has a right to be a stranger and a pilgrim in it. His ear has heard the solemn warning (which elevates, yet sinks, with a sanctifying sorrow as to all around, in the depths of the heart) : " Arise and depart: this is not your rest; it is polluted." And he takes up his cross, and sets out, solemnized, broken in spirit perhaps (it is good in such a world), but cheerfully, because he sees that Christ has gone before, and that the victory which overcomes the world is his faith. For " who is he that overcometh the world, but he that believeth that Jesus is the Son of God?" He can be himself, Christ being his life, in a world of evil and confusion, not conformed or belonging to it; not formed by it in motive or principle of life (though naturally as to mere outward circumstances not uninfluenced by it), but acting in it according to his own; happy to have companions in the excellent of the earth, but a Leader and a Lord in Christ. By this he judges of everything. He has seen perfection in Christ, and he is led by it. Greece and Rome were all judged by that. The assimilating power is one only—Christ—God manifested in flesh; folly to the world, of course. But he knows whom he has believed; he has no doubt as to the excellency of the object and model, nor of its absoluteness and completeness. The Christian believes that Christ gave Himself for our sins to redeem from this present world. Let not man tell me that meant the heathen world. What world was Greece and Rome?

But I must lead you to notice some particulars which show further the shallowness and superficiality of this school. " The conviction of the unity and spirituality of God was peculiar," we are told, " to the Jews among the pioneers of civilization." You see how they never get beyond this point: man (not the God-man) improving, exalting self. It is deplorable. But it is another point I must refer to now. "To every Jew, without exception, Monotheism was equally natural." This with purity "are the cardinal points of education. The idea of Monotheism out-tops all other ideas, in dignity and worth. The spirituality of God involves in it the supremacy of conscience, the immortality of the soul, the final judgment of the human race."

W. You surely do not object to that.

H. Patience, good friend. In the main, though Monotheism be a poor word, I do not. But, you know, these good people have other elements of instruction. You know, too, that Babylon was a cup of prostitution (as idolatry is justly called in Scripture) for all nations; that Babylon and Jerusalem stand as the two seats of the two systems of idolatry and Monotheism. No doubt, however faithless the Jews were, it was faithlessness to a known truth; which truth was Monotheism, involving, as Dr. Temple assumes, the immortality of the soul.

W. Well, that is quite just; but what conclusions do you draw from that?

H. How was I surprised—no, I was not, from some acquaintance with these rationalist doctors, particularly superficial borrowers, as English rationalists are : I correct myself, I was not surprised—to find : " She [Asia] had been the instrument selected [!] to teach the Hebrews the immortality of the soul; for whatever may be said of the early nations on this subject, it is unquestionable [what rationalists say is always, you must understand, unquestionable], that in Babylon the Jews first attained the clearness and certainty in regard to it, which we find in the teaching of the Pharisees." It is clear, therefore, that Monotheism involves the knowledge of the immortality of the soul; for it was taught to those who held Monotheism by the most idolatrous Polytheists in the world. Is this philosophical or historical? It is unquestionable, of course.

W. Now, do not be bitter.

H. Contempt is not bitterness; yet, I admit, no human being should be despised. It is the glory of Christianity to make it impossible; but reasonings and pretensions to light and superiority of mind of this kind I may despise, and do.

See again the superficiality of such a statement as this: "The New Testament is almost entirely occupied with histories—the life of our Lord, and the life of the early Church;" and he refers to the Epistles. Now, that the New Testament does give us truth in living evidence of it, and works truth out in the actual living relationships of the soul with God, and is not dry systematic theology, I admit with all my heart; but it is exactly the use of this blessed character of Scripture to deny the truth on which these relationships are founded, which shows the excessive superficialness of this remark. That *all* the Epistles were "the fruit of the current history" I admit fully. Very often mistakes and faults were their occasion; but what then? The doctrine is grace meeting need, not treatises for the competency of the human mind. But does that say that the revelation of grace to this need was not doctrine, and doctrine of the deepest and most wonderful character? Nothing but the incapacity of apprehension which cold-hearted rationalism produces could ever have such an idea for a moment. "That early Church," we are told, "does not give us precepts, but an example"— fine words; but as stupid as they are false. They will have only man. The Church gives. God must not be brought in—must not even give. What a heartless system it is! Did God, by whatever instruments, give nothing

F

to " that Church " ? Were the epistles not given to it—not by it? Nothing, moreover, can be more false than the statement itself. There is not what Dr. Temple states, save in the smallest degree; and there is almost exclusively what he states there is not. No doubt in St. Paul, from his very nature, the letters disclose the man; but the epistles are entirely composed of doctrines and precepts : whoever doubts about it has only to read them. All this is theory, perfectly regardless of facts. They are all " letters for the time," and all " treatises for the future." When Dr. Temple says, " To these pages, accordingly, the church of our day turns for renewal of inspiration," though somewhat acquainted with the pretensions of rationalism, I confess I can hardly understand it, unless it be a very common-place fact put in a bombastic way, to exalt men now to a level with the apostles, make the epistles a mere aroused energy of man, reference to which may arouse energy in us. They " turn for renewal of inspiration." I ask you, what does that mean?

W. Well, I really do not know. I remember Balaam went to seek enchantments : perhaps it is that in a good sense.

H. I know of no such going to God for inspiration in Scripture. There is inquiring of the Lord. That, in the modesty of Scripture—and how lovely it is in everything! —I can understand; and that a man taught of God, reading Scripture may be animated, his soul refreshed and filled with the truth and Spirit of God; but " turning for a renewal of inspiration " I must leave to the high-flown pretensions of modern despisers of revelation. I remember once speaking to the very chief of this system in a foreign country, one who has largely spread it among evangelical men. He denied inspiration as held in the common belief of the Church of God. I said to him, "You speak of avoiding the question of the inspiration of the Old Testament. That is a very easy way of avoiding the difficulties of your subject, you who deny inspiration in the vulgar use of the word: because the Lord and the apostles plainly declare the Old Testament to be inspired." "O yes," he said—declining to answer as to the Lord, as he had already given too much scandal by it—"no upright, honest man can deny that the apostles treat the Old Testament as inspired, and quote it as such, but they deceived themselves." He said this with an *aplomb* that was inconceivable. I only said, "Then it is a question as to your or the apostles' competency and authority as to Christianity. That is soon settled." And so I must say to Dr. Temple, if he turns to biographical Scripture for a renewal of himself. He must forgive me, if I still trust somewhat more to the old inspiration than to the renewal of it—more to the Divinely-given teaching of those who were sent by the Lord and by the Holy Ghost, and fitted for this work, and separated to it, and who could say "He that is of God hears us;" and "if any man be spiritual, let him acknowledge that the things that I write unto you are the commandments of the Lord; and if any be ignorant, let him be ignorant." He who can go there for renewal of inspiration, and find only two lives there, must have a singular process of blinding himself.

Remark too the assiduous confounding what is Divine and human. "The age of reflection begins. . . . The spirit or conscience comes to full strength; and assumes the throne intended for it in the soul." Be it so, though the confusion of the spirit and the conscience is a mischievous one, as we may see. But mark what soon follows: " Now the education by no means ceases when

the spirit thus begins to lead the soul." "The office of
the spirit is, in fact, to guide us into truth, not to give
truth." Note here the use of scriptural terms, so as to
humanize and destroy their force: the spirit is first conscience; it is grown up at the age of reflection, and takes
its seat on the throne; then it guides into truth. This in
the Scripture is said of the Holy Ghost, the Comforter,
who was to be sent down from heaven, who was to show
them the things of Christ. Here the spirit, which was
just now conscience, guides into truth, but gives no truth.
That is, the Holy Ghost reveals nothing—shows nothing;
the Comforter is only the conscience of man.

Further, note, there are no precepts to be found. The
Holy Ghost is thus dropped into mere conscience, and no
truth is given. But let us proceed in the description of
this state of full age. "He is free, but freedom is not
the opposite of obedience, but of restraint." "The law,
in fact, which God makes the standard of our conduct,
may have one of two forms. It may be an external law—
a law which is in the hands of others, in the making, in
the applying, in the enforcing of which we have no share
—a law which governs from the outside, compelling our
will to bow, even though our understanding be enlightened or not. . . . Or, again, the law may be an
internal law; a voice which speaks within the conscience,
and carries the conscience along with it; a law which treats
us, not as slaves, but as friends, allowing us to know what
our Lord doeth; a law which bids us yield, not to blind
fear or awe, but to the majesty of truth and justice; a
law which is not imposed on us by another power, but by
our own enlightened will." Remark here how all subjection to God, or authority of God, is wholly denied. But
this all gets a distinct character, uniting the first and last

quoted passages by words in a previous page describing this time of full age. "Thus the human race was left to itself, to be guided by the teaching of the spirit within."

Now I hold, as you know, that a Christian is not under law at all; he is dead to the law by the body of Christ. But it is one of the characteristics of modern rationalism, to take certain advances in truth, which the Church at large does not see, and to pervert them to evil. Here the conscience and spirit are identified; and the spirit gives no truth, but guides into it (that is, it is man's growing up into it); but there is no *revealed* truth. There is a life, an example, we are allowed "to know what our Lord doeth." The human race is left to itself, to be guided by the teaching of the spirit within, which is only conscience. But it is left to itself; no truth given, no precepts ever found in the word; and in addition to all this the *authority* of God wholly set aside. The law we have is this conscience or spirit within—is not a law imposed on us by another power, but by our own enlightened will: we bow to the majesty of truth and justice, to God never. He may neither give truth nor impose a command. God's word—His precepts, the Spirit giving any truth, the authority of God, obedience—is wholly denied.

Now the scheme of Christianity is the opposite of this. It teaches of a Comforter, the Holy Ghost, who is sent by Christ from the Father, whom the Father sends in Christ's name, who comes and convinces the world. He testifies of Christ, and the disciples also bear witness. He does not speak of Himself, but what He hears He speaks. He was to teach the disciples all things, to show them things to come, to bring what Christ had said to their remembrance; and he who loved Him would keep His commandments. Now this Christianity of the apostle John, these

words of Christ, every honest man must see, are contrary
to and contradictory of Dr. Temple's statements. He may
think that he knows Christianity and Christ's teaching
better than John. His opinion of himself in that respect
I cannot doubt; but that his is the opposite of apostolic
teaching is most evident. I prefer apostolic accounts of
Christianity. Dr. Temple may think his conscience, and
his, of course, enlightened will, superior to the Holy Ghost
which Christ promised. I profess I prefer Johannean
Christianity, if we are so to call it—the commandments
of Christ—the truth taught and given by the Holy Ghost,
to the first essay which is to illustrate moral and religious
truth. It may be prejudice; it may be stupidity; but the
shining of these modern stars does not, to my spirit and
conscience, eclipse the teaching, ay, the giving of truth,
of the Holy Ghost sent down from heaven (for so the
word of God speaks). Hear the apostle, who most clearly
teaches, we are not under law as risen with Christ : " To
them that are without law, as without law. Yet not without law to God, but rightly subject (ἔννομος) to Christ."
How carefully he shows that there is subjection to God.
So John, " This is love, that we keep His commandments." So Christ Himself, " I have kept my Father's
commandments, and abide in His love ; " and in the
highest of His free acts of grace, His offering Himself,
He says, " But that the world may know that I love the
Father, and as the Father has given me commandment, so
I do." It is with us, as it was with Christ, the law of
liberty ; because the new man finds its delight both in
what is commanded and in *obedience itself*, as Christ did :
" I delight to do it; yea, Thy law is within my heart."
But we are sanctified unto obedience, the obedience of
Jesus Christ. It is not a law stopping, or attempting, for

it did not do it in fact, to stop an evil nature, but the will of God, the motive of the new man, as of Christ. It is not yielding to the majesty of truth and justice, but to God. The doctrine of the essay is the casting off wholly God's authority, the principle of revolt and apostasy; denying the Master (δεσπότην, not κύριον) that bought us, the only Lord (δεσπότην) God. The heathen were partially a law to themselves when they were ἄθεοι, atheists, in the world. This, with increased light, is what is recommended. It is a denial of redemption, of obedience, of God's authority; a denial of the Holy Ghost as giving any truth; it is merged in an enlightened will, our spirit or conscience. " That early church (i.e., the epistles) does not give us precepts even."

W. But he speaks of obedience.

H. He does, but it is "obedience to the rules of his own mind," not the child once obedient to a parent, now in direct subjection to God in love *as Christ was,* but the rules of his own mind—all he knows. Christ's delight was to keep His Father's commandments; the saint's delight is the same; the rationalist's to be left to himself, and have nothing to say to God. It is the dignified liberty of a grown man, competent to guide himself, instead of being a child.

" The church, in the fullest sense, is left to herself, to work out, by her natural faculties, the principles of her own action." Can anything more completely deny the presence of the Spirit, and the authority of the word, that is, of God in every way? What makes her the Church in this case, I am sure I do not know. It is an epoch when men have learned beauty from Greece, patriotism from Rome, the immortality of the soul from Babylon through the Jews when departed from God, seen an example in Christ and that early Church, whatever it was, and then are left to themselves to follow their own enlightened will : that is all the Church means. How the apostles blundered about the whole matter, to think that they were sent by the Lord, and laid down their lives for—I am sure I do not know what ! and were so bigoted, that they say " He that is of God heareth us, and he that is not of God heareth not us ; hereby know we the Spirit of truth and the spirit of error." Why the Spirit does not give truth at all ! What a pity Dr. Temple was not there to instruct them ! I suppose men were not ripe for it in the apostles' days. And they were obliged to be thus bigoted, or did not know any better ; and now in this advanced age we can profit by and appreciate the teaching of these men grown to full age. I wonder whether they think that they that are of God hear them ; though I do not know why they do not leave men to the *rules* within instead of writing essays.

W. I do not exactly see, to say the truth, how these men call themselves Christians, and clergymen too.

H. Oh, you see they can consent to many things they think very inexpedient. And though they have said that the Articles are not superstitious or erroneous, yet some expressions may appear so. If they have acknowledged the same to be agreeable to the word of God, some distinctions may be founded on the word " acknowledge." They have allowed them, but " we allow many things we do not think wise or useful." " He does not maintain it, nor regard it as self-evident, nor originate it. Many better and wiser men than himself have acknowledged the same thing : why should he be obstinate ? Besides, he is young and has plenty of time to consider it " (when he has signed it of course), " or he is old and continues to submit out of habit, and it would be too absurd, at his time of life, to be setting up as a church reformer."

W. But Dr. Temple does not say all this : it is not in his essay.

H. No; he only joins in publishing the volume, in the hope that it will be received as an attempt to illustrate the cause of religious and moral truth from a free handling, in a becoming spirit, of subjects peculiarly liable to suffer, etc.

But I have nothing to say to Dr. Temple. I know nothing of him but that he is master of Rugby. I have a book before me with these principles in it.

But there is a short episode in the progress of the world's education, which is somewhat curious. The progress of the patriotic Roman empire was such, that its utter decay gave occasion for the well-known swarms from the *officina gentium* to break in upon it. Now as they had neither Grecian cultivation, nor Christian enlightened will, and their patriotism was rather rough-handed, what was to be done? Why the Church instinctively, not intentionally, gave up—for herself of course, it was very gracious—gave up her full-age Christianity, in which she had been fully left to herself and her own faculties, and took up law—the only means of taming these myriads that had escaped the general education of the race—gave up Christianity, and subjected herself (that is, the whole Church under its name) to the old principle of childhood—the law, to tame these barbarians. It was more than apostolic. Paul kept his liberty, but condescended to the weak ; but the church (not "that early one," but the mediæval one) gave up Christianity for herself (of course, any duty to God or the truth was out of the question ; she followed her instinct, the rule of her own enlightened will), and "had recourse to the only means that would suit the case—a revival of Judaism." * I admit the fact : only there was a deliberate mixture of heathenism with it. How it was a progress, kind and in-stinctive as it was, it would be hard to tell. Paul had struggled hard against this kind of progress ; he thought it a falling from grace. Christ became of no avail if people did it, he thought. However, there is nothing an enlightened will and the Spirit guiding into truth, without giving any, will not do. It was, in fact, neither more nor less than the old schoolmaster come back to bring some new scholars to Christ.

"Of course, this was not the conscious intention of the then rulers of the Church ; they believed in their own ceremonies as much as any of the people at large." But this is somewhat obscure. Did they believe the legal system before they imposed it ? If so, they had set up the schoolmaster before he was needed for Clovis and his Franks ; and it was no instinct at all, but they had sunk back by their own evil instinct to law. If they were in the full light of the age of reflection and enlightened will, they must have known what they were about. This does not quite hang together. Did they get into it themselves by their instinct, or, knowing it was retrograding themselves, impose it on others as necessary, and themselves adopt the revival of Judaism ? Here I am at a loss. However, "nothing short of a real system of discipline, accepted as Divine by all alike, could have tamed the German and Celtish nature into the self-control needed for a truly spiritual religion." But then, if they accepted the school-master, they were not under it before, and must have

* Remark how infidelity always excuses popery, and sides with it in these days.

known the difference. How they accepted it as Divine
is very difficult to understand, since they had recourse to
it as the only thing that would suit the case. It was
a singular procedure. They believed it as much as the
untamed Germans, accepted it as Divine, and yet had
recourse to it, because it suited the case of the latter.
Their believing it Divine, and giving up an enlightened
will, was a self-sacrifice of an unexampled kind, rewarded
with darkness that made them think it Divine.

When are they thus to get the truly spiritual religion?
I suppose that it is not modern popery and the immaculate
conception of the virgin Mary. We have had some thousand years already to tame the German and Celtish nature
into the self-control needed for a truly spiritual religion.
The Celts are under it still perhaps. Dr. Temple thinks
the Germans have got the start of them. But then this
instinctive act of the Church assumes in the same page
quite a new character. The question arises, why the less
disciplined race—Germans or Celts (though these last had
been a good while under Roman discipline—of full age
too, for they were in the empire that was attacked)—why,
I say, they could not have learned spirituality from the
more disciplined. You see they had the spirituality, and
it was by this leap into the schoolmaster's hand out of
instinct that they accepted the unspiritual, the Judaism,
the Divine, as much as the Germans. But why was the
reverse not the case? " This may happen when the more
disciplined is much the more vigorous of the two, but the
exhausted state of the Roman empire had not such strength
of life left within it. There was no alternative, but that
all alike should be put under the law to learn the lesson
of obedience."

The more disciplined, the Church, had then the spirituality to teach, but had recourse to a revival of Judaism as the only means which could suit the case. Still it was not the conscious intention of the Church. They believed in the Divine character of what they had recourse to. And do you see the reason of this astonishing mystification of having recourse to a thing as the only means suited to this case, yet without any conscious intention, yet possessing the spirituality which would show what it was? It was the state of exhaustion of the Roman empire, and that is progress. How charming is Divine philosophy! They retrograde out of spirituality to Judaism, *reculent pour mieux sauter*, I suppose, to begin the progress over again. But alas! there is no good in meddling with low principles. They believed they were Divine; they who were of the full reflective age had to be put themselves under the law to learn the lesson of obedience. Who put them, God knows; but why had they, the spiritual ones, to be put under law, when they had already learned obedience of a far higher kind, and were disciplined and had spirituality to teach, only that the others needed the law?

Ah, the truth will leak out in spite of theories; the professing Church, like man in all states, progresses backwards. What is perfect in its place is given of God first, and man corrupts it; so did Adam innocent, so did Noah, so did Israel under law, so did the priesthood, so did the royalty, so did the Church under grace. The whole of this statement is a wilful perversion of history: the progress of darkness and superstition, and the legal spirit, and of hierarchical and then monarchical power, is as notorious and well known as possible. The inroad of barbarians gave politic Rome the means of reducing it into a governmental system under Hildebrand. But the

corruption itself had been growing from the time the
mystery of iniquity began to work, and was ripened by
degrees into the Papacy, which partially supplanted the
empire by an influence of a new kind. But that the
Church had to be put under law to learn the lesson of obedience, though thus laboriously obscured by inconsistent
statement, is the admission that it had utterly fallen from
its first estate. That going back to law was an advance
towards spirituality, no true Christian will think a moment
in presence of Paul's statements. The return to law was
the corruption of Christianity, mingled, and *avowedly*
mingled, with heathenism as it was. The rulers of the
Church used this with a perfectly conscious intention, as
the mission of Augustine to England proves, to bring
them under their own hierarchical power. History shows,
too, that, as to the first great inroad of barbarians, its
whole history was different; the Goths were Arians; and
the theory, confused as it is, has no historical ground at
all.

W. Are you sure that you do not take a one-sided view
as to a previous point? Is not Dr. Temple merely insisting upon the use of revelation as light rather than as a
law; and while insisting on one point as that which he
feels important, not denying the use of revelation, only
urging the spirit in which it is to be used? A somewhat
exclusive one-sided view is natural, when we are absorbed
by one view of a subject important at the moment.

H. Your question is a very fair one. We all are liable
to such excess in reasoning, if not very watchful. But my
answer is very simple; and it shows that all this train of
reasoning is a dead set at revelation; that is, an effort
with unconscious intention, perhaps instinctive, as the
only means which would suit the case. Dr. Temple says,

" If they could appeal to a revelation from heaven, they would still be under law; for a revelation speaking from without, and not from within, is an external law and not a spirit." Is not this as plain as plain can be, that progress means emancipation from revelation? You see, too, what a spirit is. God, any expressed authority of God, or given truth, must be absolutely excluded; it is the childhood of law.

W. It is fatally plain. I had no idea it came to this. It is not even Deism.

H. It is remarkable that a friend of mine once heard Mr. Powell (now no more, I believe) preach; and he said, " It is in vain they seek to escape mysteries. They must become Atheists, for the greatest mystery is the existence of God." What loss there is I need not say. The Lord says, that the Holy Ghost, the Comforter, which should come, should take the things that were His, and show them to them; and all that the Father has is His, all the infinitude of the unseen heavenly, and, I may say, Divine world, was to be revealed, and that in the intimacy of the relationship of the Father and the Son, so that we should have fellowship with them. And no man had gone up there, but He who descended thence. He could speak what He knew, and testify what He had seen—declare the Father as in His bosom. He and He only had seen the Father; but this is truth given by the Spirit (all of it, even what Christ said). All of it is lost by this system. Instead, we are to have the spirit or conscience assume the throne intended for him in the soul, and draw from the storehouse of youthful experience, and legislate upon the future, without appeal, except to himself—a law which is not imposed upon us by another power, but our own enlightened will. All that God can give of the heavenly blessedness of the Son, now a glorified man, is lost, for ever lost; and man is only to seek the development of what is within man.

W. It is, indeed, a loss—a strange progress! It is inconceivable to me how any who respect Christianity, can put their sons under the influence of such principles.

H. Alas! my friend, the greater part of the world, and particularly the upper classes, go with the stream; and if God, in chastisement, sees fit to let loose Satan's influence, they float with circumstances. The air—I use it only metaphorically—is darkened with the smoke of the pit. And this rejection of objective religion is as unphilosophical as it is unchristian; for all creatures must be formed by objects. God alone is self-sufficient. He can create objects in the display of His love; but He needs none outside Himself—a creature does. Man has no *intrinsic* resources within himself, whether fallen or unfallen; nor even angels. Take away God, what are they? Nothing, or devils.

So man: if money is his object, he is avaricious, or covetous at any rate; if power, ambitious; if pleasure, a man of pleasure; and all other objects are judged of by the ruling one. In every case of a creature, what is objective is the source of the subjective state. In Christianity this is connected with a new nature, because the old *will* not have the Divine object which characterizes and is the foundation of faith; but the principle remains unchanged. "We all, with open [unveiled] face, beholding the glory of the Lord, are changed into the same image from glory to glory, as by the Spirit of the Lord." See what a magnificent picture we have in Stephen of this? —in a remarkable way, no doubt; but still exhibitory of it morally, as well as by a vision. The whole question between Christianity and Dr. Temple's system is brought to an issue. The progress of human nature, with the very elements he speaks of, and the contrasted result, is stated. "Ye do always resist the Holy Ghost: as your fathers did, so do ye." There is the relationship between man and the Spirit. Next, "Which of the prophets have not your fathers persecuted? and they have slain them which showed before of the coming of the Just One, of whom ye have been now the betrayers and murderers." These were their ways with those who unfolded the law in a more spiritual manner, and with the great living witness of perfection Himself. Such was man—flesh in contrast with the law. Such was his state : he always resisted the Holy Ghost. Now note the contrast of the objective spiritual man. Stephen, "full of the Holy Ghost, looked up steadfastly into heaven, and saw the glory of God and Jesus standing at the right hand of God, and said, I see the heavens opened, and the *Son of man* standing at the right hand of God." And what was the effect, the subjective effect, in one full of the Holy Ghost, of his objective perception of heavenly objects? In the midst of rage and violence, and while being actually stoned, in all calmness* he not merely bears, but kneels down, and says, "Lord, lay not this sin to their charge." So Jesus : "Father, forgive them ; for they know not what they do." Then he said, "Lord Jesus, receive my spirit ;" as Jesus had said, "Father, into Thy hands I commend my spirit."

---

* The same calmness marks his whole discourse. He recites the Jews' history, their own boast, so that they could have no word to say ; yet it said all. They had rejected Moses the true deliverer, Joseph their sustainer and help; and the temple they had trusted in, God had rejected by the mouth of their prophets.

He beheld, with unveiled face, the glory of the Lord, and was changed into the same image from glory to glory, as by the Spirit of the Lord. But how full and complete a picture!—man always a resister of the Holy Ghost; under law, not keeping it; with prophets, persecuting; with the Just One, a murderer; with the witness of the Holy Ghost, gnashing his teeth and slaying in rage. Christianity, in contrast—a man full of the Holy Ghost, seeing Jesus the Son of man in heaven, changed into His image, and killed by man, falls asleep, Jesus receiving his spirit.

Dr. Temple goes over this ground, rejects Christianity as an external revelation (that must be a law), takes up exactly the same elements as Stephen, and declares that man is progressively educated by them to do without that which Stephen enjoyed. Which am *I to believe?* Yet I have but coldly sketched the elements of thought. I must leave you to meditate over it, and appreciate the beauty and *spiritual* importance of it. It is a most enchanting picture, and the deepest moral principles are contained in it; but Scripture is a wonderful book.

W. But, then, this was a vision.

H. No doubt; but what he saw is revealed and written for my faith to act on.

W. True; I see plainly that Christianity judges wholly that nature which Dr. T. educates for itself—I cannot say for God. This rejection of Christ in the world made evidently a turning-point in the world's history, as to the proof of what it really was; and this history of Stephen shows man resisting the testimony to Christ's heavenly glory, as they had killed Him when He was the witness of perfection and of God on earth.

H. Just so. There is a silent witness to the Divinity of Jesus, and, while truly and really a man, a contrast

G

between Him and all other men, which has profoundly interested me. When man is blessed, morally blessed, elevated, he must have an elevated, and, indeed, to be taken out of self, a Divine object before him. Jesus was the object even of heaven, instead of having one. When Stephen is before us, heaven was open to him as it was to Jesus; but he sees the Son of man in the heavens, and that fixes his view, and lights up his regard with the glory he saw. Heaven is opened upon Jesus, and the angels are His servants; He sees it opened, and the Holy Ghost descends, witness that He is the Son of God. But He is changed into no other image by it; He has no object to which to look up, but heaven looks down to Him, and the Father's voice declares, " This is my beloved Son, in whom I am well pleased."

W. That is deeply interesting and supremely beautiful. What a word, indeed, Scripture is! I find often these traits, which, to the renewed soul, stamp the person of Jesus as Divine, more powerful as witnessing who He was, than even positive texts.

H. They are; but that does not diminish the importance of the positive texts. We enjoy these revelations of His person, but the declaration that the Word was God (and many such-like) is a declaration which has authority over my soul. I make God a liar, as John speaks, if I do not believe it; and so I can use it with others. God has declared it: he that believes not has made God a liar, because he has not believed the record which God has given concerning His Son. He that believes has the witness in himself. And all these traits which clothe, or rather reveal, the beloved person of Him who was humbled for us, are ineffably sweet; but the positive declaration is of all importance, too.

Note, in a passage I have alluded to, two other ways in which Jesus is presented, besides the actual declaration that He was God, and the Word made flesh. He gathers round Himself. If He were not God, this would be frightful—a subversion of all truth—a destructive impossibility: He would turn men away from God. He accepts this place. All that is attracted by what is good flows around Him, and finds there its perfect and all-satisfying centre. That is God. No one else could or ever did do this, except in sin or violence. The Church can say, Come and drink, I have the living water; so she has; but not, Come to me. That marks the spirit of apostasy. The stream (blessed be God!) flows there, but she is no fountain to which to go. This must be Divine, or it is false. But mark, this is a new gathering by a Divine revealed centre, not the educational progress of the race; it is the opposite, though blessed instruction for the whole race. The other way Jesus is revealed is in the words, " Follow me." We have the same perfection, but now by and in Him as man there is a path revealed through this world of evil. It is one, only one, following Christ. There can be no way but a new Divine one, yet necessarily a human one; there is no way for man, as man, in the world at all. When Adam was in paradise, he did not want a way; he had only, in blessed and unfeigned thankfulness, ignorant of evil, to enjoy good and to worship. When man has been cast out, and the world has grown up away from God—away in nature, in will, there can be no way in a rebellious world, in a sinful corrupt system, how to walk aright, as in and of the world, when its whole state is wrong. But if what is Divine comes into it as man (what has motives not of it, nor of human nature, though truly man); if it gives a path in which the Divine nature is displayed in grace and holiness in these circumstances, yet always itself manifesting what it is in them; now I have a way. I follow Him truly—in everything—a man; but a man displaying Divine qualities in the ordinary circumstances of human life. He says, " Follow me," but when He has said, " Ye are not of the world, as I am not of the world," and goes into glory, sanctifies Himself even externally, in His ascension, from the human race, that we may be sanctified by the truth. How thoroughly opposite, to be sure, Christ's system in every detail is, to Dr. Temple's!

W. It is. But what you refer to gives a scope to Christianity, and a character which elevates, indeed attracts to an object—a Divine object; yea, we may be allowed to say, attaches to it: but it shows that our ordinary Christianity is poor work indeed—I mean poor in principle. I am not comparing persons: take myself, the first.

H. It is. Yet there is more of it practically, where it could not be unfolded in terms, among the poor of the flock, than we may be aware of. Still I am sure, alas! you are right. But it is the beauty of Christianity, that, being objective, being truth, " the truth shall set you free," and a person, " the Son shall set you free," it works effectually in those who receive Christ, and requires no intellectual development to receive its power. Christ is received into the heart, and, dwelling there by faith, produces the effect in us. Yet it takes us out of ourselves, because it is objective; and we, filled with delight in an object, in what is perfect, are like Him, but so forget ourselves (and are filled by doing so), as He did in grace.

W. How skilful God is!

H. Yes; it is Divine wisdom. Man would produce

virtue by the love of virtue in himself; but then he thinks of himself, and all his virtue is rottenness. God gives us a human but Divine object, and our affections are Divine, because we love what is so (and morally we are what we love); but we love it in another, and are delivered from self. I would just add, that I believe that this adaptation of the character of walk to our entirely new position in Christ is what is meant by " created again in Christ Jesus unto good works, which God has *afore prepared* that we should walk in them." Hence we are the epistles of Christ, engraved in the fleshy tables of the *heart* by the Spirit of the living God.

W. This contrast with the Christianity of the Scriptures is, I think, what strikes one most, because it is not merely particular errors or difficulties, but evidently the whole system and principle of relationship with God, of moral influences, and the formation of the soul in God's image (and I must add, though I do not see any reference to such a thing in Dr. T.'s system, for communion with God) is in question. The whole system is the opposite of the Christian one. I must reject one, if I receive the other. They are more than contrary—they are contradictory.

H. Undoubtedly they are. The very starting-point is opposite. Christianity treats man as a fallen being, not merely as imperfect, but as departed from God, and needing a new nature and redemption. Christ meets Nicodemus at once on this ground.

The rationalist or infidel system takes in Christianity by the bye, as it does Greece and Rome; but man, as he is, is to be educated.

There are a few points it may yet be well to take notice of. Can anything prove more completely how moral intelligence is lost, or does not exist, in the minds of these teachers, than the following statement ?—" The Pharisees had succeeded in converting the Mosaic system into so mischievous an idolatry of forms, that St. Paul does not hesitate to call the law the strength of sin." Nothing can show more ignorance of the human heart or of Paul's reasonings. His principle is that " the carnal mind is enmity against God, and is not subject to the law of God, neither indeed can be." "When the commandment came, sin revived and I died ; and the commandment ordained to life became to me death." " If a law had been given which could have given life, verily righteousness should have been by the law." He sees an external *exigence* of righteousness, which imputes sin and gives no life. He goes to the very depths of our moral being ; he shows the law to be spiritual, and our flesh carnal, and takes man out of the flesh, makes him dead to the law by the body of Christ, that he may live to God. All this which ploughs up the whole moral nature by its word, " Thou shalt not lust," sinks in these eminently superficial men into the effect of a mere converting the Mosaic system into a mischievous idolatry of forms. The Lord Jesus did judge the neglect of substance for form, but, once the flesh had fully proved itself by rejecting Him (for lawless sin and law-breaking were complete when He came), then its nature is judged, instead of the law educating it. It is not subject to the law of God, neither indeed can be. And how even our hearts feel that Paul is truer, knew more about it, than the rationalists, if one morsel of spirituality be in us ! But, turn on whatever hand you will, you are met by the superficiality of these pretenders to progress. Do you think, my dear W., that grace overcomes the lusts of the flesh ?

W. So we have learnt, through mercy.

H. Not at all; "The moral toughness of the Jewish nature, which enabled them to outlive Egyptians, Romans, Mussulmans, was well matched against the baffling evil." And so it has been communicated, I suppose, to our natures, which are not tough at all. Is it not deplorable? There is only one more principle produced in this essay, but an important one of the rationalistic school, on which I would make a remark—their view of the Bible; for they boast of the Bible and of Christ in their own way. "The Bible, from its very form, is exactly adapted to our present want. It is a history; even the doctrinal parts of it are cast in an historical form, and are best studied by considering them as records of the ·time at which they were written, and as conveying to us the highest and greatest religious life at that time." It has its value "by virtue of the principle of private judgment, which puts conscience between us and the Bible, making conscience the supreme interpreter." Now that every man has a conscience is a truth of the last importance. God has taken care that man, falling into sin, should, in and with the sin, acquire the knowledge of good and evil—a profound and admirable ordering of Divine wisdom, as it was impossible he could have that knowledge before. The knowledge of good and evil, in One necessarily above all evil in nature, is the sphere of, and inseparable from, holiness. In man this is impossible. He is in innocence, or with a conscience in sin. But then if conscience come with sin, while in itself it is the knowledge of good and evil, *i.e.*, of the difference of right and wrong, it may be deadened, perverted, gives no motives more than approval and disapproval, no power, no living object, save as fear of judgment may come in.

To man in this state a revelation of God is made from the beginning, a promise of deliverance in another than himself; the all-important principle we have seen of the mind being taken out of self—affections, thankfulness, adoration of heart, introduced in contrast with judgment, while the truth of judgment is owned, law confirmed, but deliverance given from it. But God gives a full revelation as to the whole of His relationships with man, in responsibility, and in grace. That is, He either puts Himself in relationship, or shows a relationship which exists, with the being who has the conscience. We must consider it in both these lights. The latter is law, the former grace. Both were already seen in Paradise. In and out of Christianity, men have sought to reconcile them. Out of Christ they never can. But there they were, responsibility and life—a command (not knowledge of right and wrong, but a command), and free communication of life—responsibility and giving of life. Man took of the first tree, and never ate of the second. He goes out a sinner, with death on him and judgment before him—the promise of a deliverer, but in another (no promise *to* him, for he was in sin, but *for* him), the Seed of the woman, which Adam specifically was not. The first creature, man, flesh, was no longer in communion, or heir—he was lost. Then came God's witness to men, and temporal judgment of the world on that footing (*i.e.* the flood); then promise unconditional, again confirmed *to* the Seed, to that one only, as Paul says, and as is strictly and profoundly true (Gen. xxii.). No question of responsibility is raised; God would bless all nations in the promised Seed. But could the question of righteousness be left as indifferent? Impossible. It is raised by law, obedience and blessing, disobedience and the curse. This is broken before it is formally given in its first and chiefest link—that which bound man immediately to God. They made other gods —turned their glory into the similitude of a calf eating hay. Then, after various dealings in mercy, and Christ presenting Himself to the world's responsibility, the work of God comes, not dealing *with* the responsibility of men, but recognising it; grace, which brings salvation, sealing the truth of all the previous responsibility (for otherwise salvation were not needed), but going on another ground and meeting the case. Christ takes the effect of the broken responsibility on Himself, dies for sin, and is the source of life, and that according to righteousness. The whole question of the two trees of paradise (life-giving, and good and evil, and man's ruin in this) is settled, for those who receive Christ, for ever, with the largest—yea, a perfect—revelation of God as Father, Son, and Holy Ghost, in all His riches and ways.

Two points come before us in what Dr. T. says:—how we are to view the Bible, even the doctrinal parts of it; and conscience being between us and the Bible as supreme interpreter.

The whole question is, Is there a revelation? Is anything heavenly to come within the scope of man's thoughts? Has God to be known, or merely right and wrong discerned? And if He has to be known, must He not reveal Himself?

Now I say, if we are to be blessed, God must be known. If I am away from God in sin (and so the Scripture treats man, and conscience cannot deny it), doing right and wrong cannot be settled but by returning to God. If a child has wickedly abandoned his father's house, he may leave off particular faults, but he can never be right till he returns and submits to his father. But the true know-

ledge of God is lost, and the more man reasons in sin, the
more it is lost. It will be said, God must be good. I can
say this when once He has been revealed; for heathens
did not know this as truth, though instinct looked for it—
wants looked for it: but they did not in their notion of
God rise above the passions of men. When they did rise
above them, they held that God could have nothing to say
to men. But now God has been revealed, even the poorest
man knows God must be good. But if I begin to reason,
what do I see? An innocent child perishing in agony, the
mass of the world degraded to the lowest degree by heathenism. How is He then good? An infinitesimal part
of the race for centuries alone knowing the unity of the
Godhead, and they almost worse than their neighbours;
sin having power over myself; brutality in families, wars,
tumults, and miseries—how is He good? If I say, Ah!
but that is fallen man departed from God: then I ask,
How then can he be received back again? I cannot with
any sense deny that he is a sinner; and if God did not
make him bad, he is fallen. The cravings of nature prove
he is. How can he be back with God, whom I must then
think to be holy and pure?

A revelation from God and of God is the first necessity
of my nature as a moral being. I get both in Christ.
"He whom God hath sent speaketh the words of God."
I set to my seal, on believing Him, that God is true; but
then it is not only the word received from above—that a
prophet, that John, had, and spoke of earthly things,
moved in the sphere in which God dwelt with man as a
creature on earth responsible to God; but He came Himself from above. God spoke in the Son; His words were,
in a personal and complete way, though a man, the words
of God. They were spoken by the Lord. Now he that

receives His testimony sets to his seal that God is true. And note how this is stated: " No one is ascended up to heaven, but He who is come down from heaven, even the Son of man who is in heaven," and " what He hath seen and heard that He testified." Oh! what a blessing is here, which none else can give! for none else has gone up to heaven to tell us what is there. In this poor distracted sin-beset world I have the sweet and holy ways and Divine objects of heaven brought down to my heart, by One who is the centre of its glory and delights, and come to bring them to me in love, yet without leaving it.

W. But is there not a conscience which must and does judge what is before it? For instance, if a God were revealed who was not good, or who was not holy, how could I possibly receive such a being as God?

H. How long has that been the case with man? Was there ever a case where conscience made a difficulty when a revelation had not been given? Was there ever such a thing as a holy God thought of, or the need of holiness in God dreamt of, in any religion but a revealed one? We may find partial traces of goodness as to human need and deliverance from tyranny in India, in the avatars of Vishnu, in that otherwise monstrous idolatry; but all idolatry everywhere proves that the notion that goodness and holiness were required in a Divine Being by the conscience of man is utterly false. The gods were the reproduction of men's passions with a superior degree of power. *When* revelation was given, and redemption was made known by God, then holiness and goodness were made known and estimated, but nowhere else. That is, instead of the conscience being between us and the Bible (or a positive revelation), there must be a revelation between God and us, and our conscience, or if you please, between

God and us, in order that the conscience may feel that
God must be good and holy to be God at all. When the
revelation has been given, the conscience recognises it,
but never before. Now this is essential and conclusive on
the question before us, and shows us that conscience within
is wholly incapable of judging. But there is a conscience,
and when a Divine revelation or light comes to it from God,
it is susceptible of impressions from it, so as to have a right
judgment, but never without, as to what is Divine. Modern
infidels are reasoning from the effect of Divine light to
deny its necessity. As when light comes in, the eye can
see; with none it cannot, and would never know it could.
Scripture is true; when men had the knowledge of God,
they did not *discern to retain* God in their knowledge.

W. I had not weighed these facts, or rather, I had not
thought of them; but they are true, and they certainly
put the pretensions of infidelity and of man's mind in a
very peculiar light. They are really vaunting themselves
as competent to judge Christianity; whereas the only light
they have to judge it by, they have got from it or from
Judaism. Without it man's mind sank into the grossest
idolatry and moral degradation. A revelation alone
enabled them, by revealing what God really is, and so
forming their understandings, to judge of what He ought
to be. There is another point strikes me in our conversation—how little their themes bear the test of history and
facts! They make boast of philosophy; but it is well
known that up to Socrates it was little but cosmogony,
and Plato's morality was communism, and his theology
demonism, and in truth metempsychosis. This argument
from conscience was what I felt least able to meet, for I
was conscious that an unholy God, or one that was not
good, I could not have borne for a moment.

H. You could not, I am sure, because you have a revelation. It is their great theme abroad. But it is always
useful to meet infidels on their own ground—I mean on
its untenableness. I have already referred to this. If
God is simply good, and the fall and redemption are not
God's truth, explain to me this state of this world, three-
quarters heathen, and of the other, a great part Mussul-
man or papist, and every kind of misery and degradation
dominant, and selfishness the dominant spring of all its
activities, where lusts and passions are not so. If man be
not fallen, where is God's goodness? And if God be not
good, what is? Christianity tells me man is fallen, and
reveals to me God in goodness in the midst of misery, and
redemption as an issue out of it: and the history of
man, not succeeding generations, sacrificed to rationalists'
theories of progress of the fifty-ninth century; but revelations of this goodness and deliverance for faith to lay
hold of from the day of man's fall, though the time was
not come to accomplish the thing promised.

And, allow me to ask you, if man be so competent, how
comes it there is so much difficulty and conflict and
uncertainty? Why is there so much difficulty in finding
out God? Why any question of discovering Him, if men
have not lost Him? Why men believe in Jupiter, or Siva,
etc., or Odin king of men, or Ormuzd and Ahriman, or
Khem, or a host of others which it is useless for me to
follow? Why have they such difficulty, when it is owned
God must be good and holy, in coming to Him and
walking with Him?

No; it is evident man has got away from God, many
horridly, degradingly; and that the fairest of Eve's
daughters are caring more for a pretty ribbon, and of her
sons for gold or a title, than for all which God presents to

them to win their hearts in the Son of God's sufferings, and offering up Himself in grace for them. No; man is fallen, has lost the sense of what God is, and of His love —has not his heart's delight in that which God is, or what is supremely good. Nothing proves it more than his not finding it out. God has given a conscience, but it does not judge the word: the word of God judges it. In one sense, every man must judge; but his judgment reveals him in presence of the word. A man's judgment of other things always reveals his own state. He is certainly lost, condemned, if he does not receive the word. God speaks, and gives adequate witness of who He is. "He that believeth not is condemned already." Light is come into the world. If men prefer darkness, it is not their conscience. Their will must be at work. Dr. Temple professes to believe, I suppose, that the Son of God is come. I ask, Is man bound to receive Him or not? There He is, to test every man's soul by His reception, or the contrary. It does test the soul. He has a right to judge, you tell me. If he does not receive Him, he proves himself bad, bad in will. He has to judge; but if he rejects what is perfect in goodness, his own state is shown. He is judged by his approval or disapproval of what is there, because perfection—because God manifest in the flesh— is there. Because God is speaking, woe to him who does not hearken! Yes, he has to judge. It is not his right: he is a lost creature; but he is tested by it—it is his responsibility. How he can meet it, I do not inquire here. I believe the grace of God is needed; but there is God speaking—speaking in grace. Is He received or not? The two things John speaks of, in the passage I allude to, are the words of God, and One come from above who is above all. Am I not bound to listen? am I not bound to receive? You ask me, Must I not judge whether they are His words, and whether He came from above? I answer, Yes; but you are judged by the result you come to, because God knows He has given a perfectly adapted and gracious witness; yea, that He is it. If you have rejected this, you have rejected Him, and remain in your sins and under wrath. To them that believe He is of price, as He is to God; to them that are disobedient, a stone of stumbling and a rock of offence. It is a savour of life to life, and a savour of death to death; and the presentation of the truth and words of God and of the Son of God must be so, because their present rejection is the rejection of Himself.

Talking of conscience between us and the Bible is all foolishness and nothing else.* The Bible is God's word in direct contact with us, telling to our conscience all that ever we did; that God is holy, but (blessed be His name!) that He is grace and a Saviour. What is conscience as distinct from us? It is that on which the word of God acts. If light comes (and God is light, and Christ was the light of the world), it makes all manifest, and acts on the eye. If the eye is in an ill state, it avoids the light; it does not judge the light: its state is proved by it; it judges colours, forms, and so on, by the light. But a conscience that is not "us," or a conscience between us and God, is an utter delusion. Conscience is the know-

---

* It is really a question between faith and infidelity. If I believe the Bible to be the word of God, the judgment is formed; I have only to bow. If I reject it, I am an infidel; my judgment of it is formed. I may be ignorant of it, then there is no judgment to be formed; though I am sure, if a new nature be in us, it will be received by us as light is by the eye, and known. The rejection of the word, it being what it is, is the judgment of what rejects it.

ledge of good and evil in us: that it is, without any further revelation of God. It has the sense of responsibility, and, though obscurely, of judgment and the consequences of sin (at any rate, as far as vague fear goes). But if Christianity be true *at all*, the Son of God has come, and speaks God's words. The moment He is received (that is, that there is faith in Him), the first judgment of conscience and heart is to bow to Him; the first right thing (for right is the just maintenance of the duties of relationship) is to listen, and obey that word; the most essentially wrong thing is not to bow and receive His word. To judge God, when I know it is Him, is the height of sin.

If Dr. Temple or these rationalists *do not believe that He has come and spoken*, I will seek to prove to their consciences that He has. There is God's way of doing it. They must judge whether He be come. To be sure; but this I tell them with certainty, from His own lips, that He is come, and if they do not believe in Him, they are condemned; if they do, they have eternal life. But if He be there, if they do believe He has spoken, their part is to listen to Him, not to judge Him. With the blinding of conscience by passions, ignorance, education, it is of the utmost importance to have a sure witness of God's mind, not dependent on the varying views of man. If I lose the Bible, I lose communications from God; I am infinitely, irreparably sunk. Dr. Temple, it seems, does not like God's word—does not like He should reveal Himself. If he has a professed revelation, he "likes to consider it as records of the time at which they were written, and as conveying to us the highest and greatest religious life at that time." That man should be developed, that may be allowed; religious life, that too; but communications from God—no. Now there have been such—God's word spoken in this world, or Christianity is all a falsehood from beginning to end, a holy imposture! which there is nothing like in the world. But if there have been such, have we lost them for ever? Are we returned to darkness? for since the true light shone—shone in one speaking the words of God, am I to have them no more, no more this revelation from God, no more any communication from Himself as such? I have lost all that was precious and elevating in the world; I have lost communication with God. I may speculate about Him—may know something of right and wrong, but I have lost all communications from Him—wretched man that I am! What was man when he had not it? What is man when he has not it?

To reduce Divine communications to apostolic life is to show a will not to hear God directly, not to have to say to Him—a dislike to have to do with the words of His mouth. It is not, " Thy words were found, and I did eat them, and they were to me the joy and rejoicing of my heart." If God have spoken, and if we deny it, we are infidels; to exalt the conscience of *man above it*, as a judge, is to set corrupt sinful man above the authority of God. I read that the word discerns the thoughts and intents of the heart. It makes its truth and the authority of God known by its action in the conscience; it tells a man all that ever he did; but it reveals a God of grace—not that the conscience judges the word. Christ did speak the words of God. Are they lost to us? If I have them, is my conscience to be between me and them! What profound nonsense such a sentence is! If you do not know them, I will not call you an infidel, but you are an unbeliever. You have not yet set to your seal that God is true. Do

H

not, at any rate, pretend to teach others, when you admit that God has spoken, and you cannot yet tell what is His word, and what is not.

W. I am glad you spoke of this question, for it is one of the practical difficulties to my mind in their way of speaking; because I feel I have a conscience, and yet I recognise the Supreme authority of the word.

H. But do you not see, my good friend, that the whole object is to get rid of revelation, and its authority over us? If God has spoken, if there be a revelation, would not the first act of conscience be to turn and bow to it—of the heart to delight in what God has revealed? for He has surely revealed Himself.

W. Of course it would be the proof that there was conscience in activity, and not will, a heart to taste the blessedness One alone can tell of.

H. That is the very point, at least a very principal one; and it is connected with the fall, which is always ignored in this system. There are two parts of conscience: one, the knowledge of right and wrong; the other, sense of responsibility, and that to God. The first, sin has practically greatly darkened; the last, will resists, though it cannot deny. The word of God comes in, gives perfect light to the conscience, and much more, and presents the authority of God to the will. Men plead conscience as a competency against God and His word, saying they must have conscience supreme. God will settle that question, whether His light and word is perfect for conscience, His authority in it sufficient to claim obedience and submission. A child has departed wickedly from its father's house, and thrown off his authority. He professes to desire to go right; his father sends a message, yea, comes and speaks to him, communicating to him his mind, and will, and grace.   He replies, " Oh, all that is a thing external to me; the real thing is the inward disposition in me."   My answer to him is, " All very fair, my good lad; but the trial and test of your disposition is your submitting to your father's word, and receiving and bowing with a thankful heart to his testified kindness."

W. But suppose he were to say, But I must know if it be my father's word.

H. All quite right.   But I reply, If your heart were right, you would be only too glad to know it is.   And when you say, that, even if it be, it is only an external thing, and my conscience after all must judge, I see you take your own judgment still, and do not want your father's word.   I know your disposition: your will likes to be master yet.   Besides, let me tell you, had you been staying in the house, you would be familiar enough with your father's voice and words to know them at once.   You are proving your own incapacity and evil.   If you do not receive and understand his words, you will remain without, and prove that incapacity—that is all.   If your disposition were right, rebel as you have been, a word from your father would be heaven to you, and the heart would delight in bowing to his authority; and this very readiness is the disposition which, directed towards his own words, is that which, morally speaking, gives capacity to receive them; for the heart is right, and the will broken. If any man will (desire, be willing) to do my will, he shall know of the doctrine whether it be of God, or whether I speak of myself.   If you talk of your conscience being supreme, when your father has spoken, it is quite clear that you wish to be independent of your father; the first proof of the true return of heart and conscience is the self-subjection to your father's declared mind and will.

You are not returned to him yet. Your whole place is wrong, conscience and all.

There is the knowledge of right and wrong as a faculty without God; but where God speaks, conscience is proved by bowing to it. See Saul: "I thought *I ought* to do many things contrary to the name of Jesus of Nazareth, which thing also I did." There was conscience. Once he has to do with the Lord, once he is right, it is "Lord, what wilt thou have me to do?" "Speak, Lord, for thy servant heareth." All short of this is alienation from God. A conscience that wants to be away from God, to judge for itself, is not an upright conscience. It is will and sin. Conscience is not only judgment, it recognises the authority of God (we are sanctified to obedience) and loves it, because it is true conscience, and the will of independent self is given up, the soul restored to God. For the word has authority as well as light. It tests the truth of conscience by giving light, but it speaks with the authority of God. Hence the Lord says, The word that I speak unto you, the same shall judge you in the last day. Judge it now, if you dare. I do not believe in the conscientiousness of a man who pleads his conscience against the word of God.

See how the apostles speak: "If we receive the witness of men, the witness of God is greater: he that believeth not God hath made Him a liar." "He that heareth my word hath everlasting life," says Christ. "Why do ye not understand my speech? Because ye cannot hear my word." "Because I tell you the truth, ye believe me not." "He that sent me is true, and I speak to the world those things I have heard of Him." "As my Father hath taught me, I speak these things." Because man has abandoned God on his original created ground, God has sent the testimony of heavenly things to bring him to a higher relationship with Himself.   And he—the wretched sinner—tells me he must listen to conscience, because this revelation is an external thing !   To be sure heavenly things, and the record of them, are very external to him. He has told the truth.   He is out of Paradise.   This world is the scene which has grown up in man's exclusion from God, who comes with the revelation of what is Divine and heavenly to bring him out of that, and into what is heavenly ; and he puts it off, and says it is external to him.   He is right.   Only if he does not receive it, *he* will be external to *it*.   He will have a conscience too : he is all right in that, and it will tell him what he has done, when the time of gracious reception is past.   His sheep hear His voice.   " But ye," says the Lord, " believe not, because ye are not of my sheep."

The word and confirming works are given, adequate testimony is given.   Woe to him who does not receive it ! He will die in his sins, and the same *word* will judge him in that day.   If God has come and spoken and revealed Himself from heaven, and we do not receive it, He and all that is heavenly is external to us, and there is nothing but self within.   But even in this notion they only show their ignorance; for " he that believeth on the Son hath the witness in himself."   The measure of the conscience becomes Divine, which natural conscience never can be, even when it is right—it must and ought to be human; whereas, when born of God through the word, on receiving the word I receive Christ, the revelation of God, and of what is heavenly.   He is my life, He is within; and I am called on to be an imitator of God as a dear child, and walk in love as Christ has loved us, so that I am, if needed, to lay down my life for the brethren ; for Christ has thus proved His love to us. My measure of conscience is Divine, acting because I have both seen and received what is Divine in receiving Christ by His word. So that, speaking of its fulness, the apostle is not afraid to say, filled with (up to) all the fulness of God. Hence, John says, " which thing is true in him and in you; because the darkness is past, and the true light now shineth." And all this heavenly revelation of and by Him, who came down from heaven, I am to give up, to have patriotism from the selfish and treacherous Romans, whose patriotism was the deceitful oppression of the world; and to learn that courage, which I may find in a cock or a bull-dog, has been ignorantly forgotten by Paul ! It is hard to have patience with such contemptible stuff.

W. But we ought.   The Master you speak of had.

H. You are right.   He was perfect in everything, and fleshly and unchristian feeling is apt ever to mingle itself with our state in such cases.   Still though we are imperfect in it, indignation in itself is not wrong in such cases.

W. But there is still a question which I should like to put to you here.

H. Well, do so.

W. I enter into your feelings as to Christ.   He whom God had sent spoke the words of God, and he who received His testimony set to his seal that God is true—an immense principle evidently every way.   I see plainly that, in receiving the word—the very name given to Christ in this respect, I receive truth, submit to Divine authority, am restored to God, enter in a heavenly way into a new relationship with Him, according to that which is revealed, and know grace, and indeed glory.   But then the apostle's words—how can I regard them ? because the personal *speaker* is, so to speak, lost.

H. As regards Christ Himself, the ineffable loveliness of all He said and did, of course, necessarily bears the stamp of heaven, of one who came thence, and yet could say who *is* in the bosom of the Father—who spoke what He knew, and testified what He had seen. This is necessarily wanting in the subsequent communication; but, on the other hand, there is gain. "It is expedient for you that I go away; for if I go not away, the Comforter will not come; but if I go I will send Him unto you." Besides the perfect expression of Divine good in Christ on earth, the question of good and evil was settled for ever. Christ being made sin, and God perfectly glorified by His offering of Himself, and His being the sin-bearer, the question of good and evil was morally settled. Thereupon man takes a place in heaven. This was a new thing. Thus you will find that characteristically (for, of course, the same truths are found in both) John gives us the Divine thing, the heavenly thing— God Himself manifested upon earth; Paul, on the ground of sovereign grace, man brought righteously into heaven. Now Christ must have suffered, risen from the dead, and gone to heaven, to have this before us, and the message or testimony of it given. Yet it must be Divine testimony to have any value; and that I have through the Holy Ghost sent down.

W. You mean, that the New Testament gives us a witness and a record, with, of course, many accessory truths, of the Divine—God Himself, θεότης, as well as θειότης, manifested in man; and man brought in a new and heavenly way completely to God.

H. I do. The former, as to its fruit in us, takes the character of life; the latter of righteousness (but Divine life—that eternal life which was with the Father, and was manifested to us, and by which, Christ being our life, we now live; and Divine righteousness). It is thus wholly a new thing—a life that was with the Father before the world was, manifested in Jesus, communicated to us—not in Adam innocent more than in Adam a sinner.

W. But, then, this becomes a kind of independent life —at any rate, once it is received.

H. In no way. The character of this life, even in Jesus as man, was the perfection of the condition in which God has given to us eternal life, and that life is in His Son. "He that hath the Son hath life." It was obedience and dependence, and a constant heavenly regard. He was the ἀρχηγὸς and τελειωτὴς of faith, a Man with His eye always out of Himself on God. So with us. When I say Christ lives in me, I must add always, "the life which I live in the flesh, I live by the faith of the Son of God, who loved me, and gave Himself for me." Divine life in a creature nature is always objective; that is its essential excellence, as indeed we have already seen.

W. Let me ask you what place you give Peter then?

H. What there is of connection in this life with the previous ways of God he pursues. It is government; and this in the strongest way confirms to me the authenticity of the second epistle. The first is government in favour of the just; the second, as regards the predominant and licentious wicked. Hence he goes to the consuming of all things in the stability of which they rest. The saint for him is a pilgrim. The great fact of redemption, of course, is fully stated for this. But we are not risen with Christ, but He is risen, and we have a living hope through His resurrection; meanwhile the government of God is displayed in favour of His people upon earth. This evidently connected it with the Old Testament, though on new ground. Hence the quotation of the thirty-fourth Psalm, " He that will love life," etc.

W. Have you ever thought of the likeness of Jude and 2 Peter? There is something strange in it.

H. How it came about may be a difficulty—perhaps a difficulty never to be solved, as many such external questions, after eighteen hundred years—interesting in their place, but immaterial. But the difference as to Divine teaching in them is clear and important. Peter speaks of wickedness, and God's dealings with it as such, God's government, as I said: Jude of apostasy or leaving the first estate, going briefly through all the characters of this, angelic, the natural man, ecclesiastical, and final rebellion against Christ, on which actual judgment will come; especially, of course, tracing it as regards the Church from false brethren first creeping in, till Christ comes to judge ungodly men. Thus Peter speaks of angels that sinned; Jude of angels that kept not their first estate, but left their own habitation. Thus Scripture fills all parts of moral truth up. Like a dissected map, it proves its own perfectness.

In the gospels, which these ignorant wise men are talking about, as to be harmonized and compared, and synoptical and supplementary, we get in Matthew Christ presented to the Jews, Emmanuel, Messiah, and the result of His rejection, but still referring to the Jews (hence no ascension); in Mark, Christ the servant prophet; in Luke, Christ the Son of man in grace, leaving them, on going to heaven, under the blessing of His thence outstretched hand (that is, the various revelations of Christ on earth as man); and in John, out of all dispensational relationship, Christ, God manifest in flesh, the Word and Son, and Divine life displayed, and the giver of the Comforter, but even here no ascension because it is not man in heaven, but God on earth. Hence we shall find another distinct characteristic of John. The three so called synoptical gospels present Christ to the responsibility of man to receive Him. In John He is seen unknown or rejected in the first chapter, and becomes the Divine object of Divinely given faith to those born of God, the Holy Ghost the Comforter being given on His going away. Were we to enter into details, we should only find this admirably, and of course perfectly, brought out. I confess when I read rationalistic views of the books (I do not mean, of course, criticism of the text, though even this be influenced by their state), I am astounded at their absolute moral incapacity. External it is to them, sure enough; at least, all that is in it, all that is Divine. They have hit here on the right word, condemned out of their own mouth.

W. But as we are speaking of this, what do you make of James?

H. It is equally admirable in its place; not a high revelation of what is Divine, but the fruit of the patient and perfect grace of God towards us. When Paul had been in the third heaven, after all he was a poor mortal; and as, speaking reverently, God had put him in the danger, though by blessing, He sent him a corrective. It was Paul's evil, no doubt, that needed it; but it was God's own goodness, which thinks of all our evil in grace, that sent it. And Paul, as you may see, got profit and advantage through it (that is, as an occasion). Now I do not say that James' epistle is a thorn in the flesh, but it is an excellent corrective of it; it is a girdle about the loins. Our loins are girt about with truth by it; the exceeding high and heavenly truth into which we are brought; the elevation to which faith brings us; its being faith (that is, a principle which takes us out of ourselves to rest on what is in God and His revelation) might lead us, not by its own nature, but by our utter perverseness, like Paul, not to be out of the flesh as it ought, but to be puffed up in it—to use liberty for a cloak of licentiousness. It is dreadful it should be so; but such we are, poor wretched creatures that we are.

James, that is really, God, comes in and meets us, and with an appropriate moral energy which is mighty in the conscience, shows that the real power of faith connects it with life. Its reality is *shown*—that is the testing word—by its fruits. And no one speaks of this as more of sovereign grace than he, in all its Pauline excellency, so as to show the connection. "Of his own will begat He us, that we might be a kind of first-fruits of His creatures." He too connects it with the law of liberty—that is, when the nature, the new man, and the prescribed will, go together. If I command my child to go where he longs to go, and tell him the way, it is obedience; but it is the law of liberty. He speaks of three laws, or law in three ways. First, the law as such—here, if guilty in one point, guilty of all. The authority of the law given has been despised in the point in which lust was active. We are wholly guilty. Secondly, the royal law of subjective perfection: Thou shalt love thy neighbour as thyself. That is doing well. Thirdly, the perfect law of liberty into which I look; that is, the revelation of the path of the Divine nature, of which I am made partaker. Revelation shows me the perfection of it, the Divine nature gives me the delight in it. I am as a present thing blessed in the doing it.

That James speaks purely of fruits of faith in justifying by works is evident from the fact that the examples he takes were no examples of the fruit of natural conscience at all. One was a father slaying his son, the other a harlot betraying her country. I do not know what the Romans or Dr. Temple would have said to her. But one was giving up everything, even the promises according to flesh, to God, in absolute obedience, counting on Him even to have Isaac again, according to His word; the other identifying herself with the Lord's people when they had not yet gained one victory in Canaan over their mighty enemies. No one pierces more deeply by the word than James into the principles and workings of the human heart, or takes grace and faith as all; but he will have it real and practical, not speculative knowledge. And we need this, and delight in it, if true of heart. Nothing showed more the really weak side of Luther than his calling this an epistle of straw. And I have no doubt at all that it greatly hindered him entering into the blessed excellences of Paul himself. But you have led me away from our subject.

W. I do not know that I have. The natural flow of our delights in Divine things is itself a testimony, and a powerful one. Besides, I apprehend, the positive production of what is good is an argument for it (it makes its very beauty), as well as, at least as strong as, mere reasonings against objections.

H. Well, I believe so; besides it keeps charity alive as regards those who do not taste them, which there is danger that reasonings which occupy themselves with evil may not do. You cannot be filled with the blessedness that is in Christ and the word, without both loving the persons of those who are simply wrong, and desiring they might partake of them. There are adversaries. This is somewhat different. There is such a thing as righteousness as regards wilful evil, and it is charity; but we have to watch ourselves close as regards this. If you saw a deliberate sinner seeking to corrupt a young practically guileless mind, would you not be indignant, and charitably indignant?

W. I should.

H. It is not reflective but it is right, and a high kind of right. It shows a soul living in what is right and caring for it. Seeing the connection between souls and God, which the other is disturbing or hindering, a millstone about such a one's neck and casting into the sea would be better for a man than his so doing; and that is felt. How far these rationalists are thus guilty I leave to God.

But to turn to our subject—the word of the apostles as compared with Christ. 2 Corinthians v. states the change from one to the other. God was in Christ, reconciling the world unto Himself, not imputing their trespasses unto them. There was the direct witness of God Himself in the person of His Son in grace; and when asked who He was by the Jews, He refers to His word: ἀρχήν, in principle, utterly and entirely, what I am saying to you (or, as in the English, " from the beginning "). His words expressed Himself. Then we have a third point, committing unto us the ministry of reconciliation. " Now then we are ambassadors for Christ, as though God did beseech by us, we pray in Christ's stead, be ye reconciled to God; for He hath made Him to be sin for us, who knew no sin, that we might be made the righteousness of God in Him."

God had Himself in Christ testified perfect grace in

His words and ways with man—revealed what was heavenly as one who had come down from heaven, and was the Son of man who was in heaven. It was the blessed, gracious revelation of what was heavenly to men, meeting all their wants and sorrows withal. But man would none of it. "No man receiveth His testimony." He then accomplishes the work which was to bring His redeemed into heaven. "Father, I will that they whom Thou hast given me be with me where I am;" and He goes to prepare a place for them. But thus His ministry by the word was closed, and He, having secured everlasting righteousness and the glory of God in their admission, sends down the Holy Ghost to be to earth a witness of it in chosen vessels, and, practically, in all who should receive their testimony. He tells them that it should not be they that spoke, but the Spirit of their Father who spoke in them; and so far from inferior was that testimony, that He encourages His disciples, by saying that a blasphemy against Him who spoke in it would be unpardonable, while a word against Himself as humbled might be forgiven. (Luke xii. 10-12.)

Hence John says, "He that is of God heareth us; he that is not of God heareth not us; hereby know we the Spirit of truth and the spirit of error." And the apostle Paul: "If any one be spiritual, let him acknowledge that the things that I write unto you are the commandments of the Lord." Again: "Now we have received, not the spirit of the world, but the Spirit which is of God, that we might know the things which are freely given to us of God; which things, also, we speak, not in the words which man's wisdom teacheth, but which the Holy Ghost teacheth, comparing," or, as I have no doubt is the sense, using a spiritual medium for communicating spiritual things.

That these things animated their life too is true; but where did they get them? The Holy Ghost was come down from heaven, as the Son had come down. He was to show them the things of Christ; to guide them into all truth; show them things to come. I suppose, if they lived in the things, they must have learned them somehow. What wretched pleading it is, to say it is the expression of the highest and greatest religious life of the time! To be sure it was. But where did they get the things to communicate on which they lived? What was the power in which they communicated them? Can Dr. Temple, who fancies he sees this life clearer than his neighbours—can he tell us anything he has not got from their revelations? He, we may hope, is living on what they communicated; but who communicated them for him to live on? All this is shuffling about the matter to deny revelation. No one could testify of what was in heaven directly but one who came thence. Christ did, and says so; the Holy Ghost did, and communicated through suited vessels the glory of Christ and the Father's love in Him.

Thus it was. After the law, the rule of God's government on earth, the prophets showed the coming Messiah, His sufferings and glories; but it was as seeing it afar off, and recalling to the law, not announcing the kingdom as then coming—the law and the prophets were until John. By him the kingdom is preached. He goes before the face of Jehovah to prepare His way. He receives from above his testimony and place; but his testimony was of the earth, repentance, judgment, the kingdom—Messiah coming amongst them. Then Christ comes, but does not receive from heaven, but comes from heaven, and can tell directly what He has seen and knows and has heard. He is in the bosom of the Father, and can declare God; and

He does so. "No man receiveth His testimony." Man wills not what is heavenly.

But what an infinite blessing is this of which these rationalists would deprive us—the positive revelation of what is heavenly, the blessed communication of what is there above ! To talk of life and religious life is all simple nonsense. Can religious life reveal what it has never seen, the blessedness in which it has never yet been ? True religious Christian life is formed by this revelation ; and think of reducing men to mere conscience, and rejecting the revelation of what is heavenly even to conscience ! What a lowering thing it is ! No ; the Son speaks what He knows, and testifies what He has seen. It is the very essence of Christianity, and sole source of blessing. But, man being so evil as to reject it, God is not frustrated in His love; the need of it as above all is made manifest; redemption is accomplished, and thereon man takes his seat on high on the throne of God, and the Holy Ghost is sent down the witness and proof of it, and testifies of the glory he (man) is in, his relationship with God his Father, all the wisdom and glory of the counsels and work by which he is brought there; the Church's place with Christ, founding a perfected and purged conscience on the work of Christ, so that holiness is righteously connected with the entrance of a sinner into the glory he had come utterly short of. This links the heart to what is heavenly; while the testimony of the Holy Ghost is the sure foundation on which the soul can rest for the certainty of it as truthful, and thus a living enjoyment. God's will and counsel; Christ's accomplished work ; the Holy Ghost's testimony (Heb. x.); that is what gives liberty and boldness to enter into the presence of God. The Scriptures are the recorded testimony for all

times.   Ministry does not cease, but revelation does,
when all is revealed.   The word of God is completed.

W. I see the Divine system in what you say, and its
wisdom and completeness, while we have to live by faith.
But there is a question I should like to ask you in connection with this—What place do you give to criticism in
this ?

H. I use it with all my heart.   If my father had left a
will of his, copied for the various members of the family,
which we felt bound us all, in which all had an interest,
and were all subject to ; of course, in copying, some errors
might have crept in.   So in the Scriptures, the oracles of
God were committed to men (mark the expression—the
oracles of God, it is formal; that is, not mere life expressed), while Providence watched over them.   But there
was as to this the responsibility of man ; as in all God's
ways with us, there is this connection of responsibility,
and yet security by grace.   Well, errors have crept into
this will ; but we are all desirous of knowing accurately
our Father's mind, assured that it is in the will.   We
compare copies to have it as accurately given as possible.
I do so, because it has authority, absolute authority, over
me the child : had it not, I should not do so.   The mul-
tiplication of the copies which has so far multiplied occasional mistakes, *quas aut incuria fudit aut humana parum
cavit natura,* has also multiplied the certainty that the whole
will is right, and has enabled me to correct isolated errors
in each one copy by comparing it with the others.   If a
word or two remain illegible, or not to be ascertained, I
must leave that word, I lose its force, if the same disposition be not elsewhere.   But it is evident I should, if I
attached value to my Father's will as such, carefully compare all to have it exact.   This has been done by men

I

skilled in it, proving how little was uncertain, and that little affecting doctrine nowhere.

W. This I see very distinctly. The proofs of the Divine record lie elsewhere. This is mere care for its correctness because it is so estimated, in which providential care and Divine faithfulness are to be trusted, as in everything we are blessed in.

H. Just so. There is no Divine blessing but by faith, nor can be, when it passes beyond mere temporal enjoyments, and they are never divinely enjoyed but by faith. This is the necessary link between the soul of man and an unseen God. In truth it was needed when He was manifested; for no man can see God, morally speaking. Therefore it was said then, " He that seeth the Son, and believeth on Him, hath everlasting life." Were it possible to see His glory and live, it would be no moral link of the soul with Him. If man were even kept from sin by it, which *outwardly* he might, it would be no real enjoyment of Him, nor living spiritual fellowship.

I think we have pretty well exhausted the subject of this essay, and enjoyed some excursions by the way to scenes it opened out to view as we passed. Many details might be taken up, but I do not know that we should gain anything material by referring to them; such as the habits of false moral estimation introduced by the heathen apprehension of things often current. His three witnesses quarrelled, but that proves nothing, if they had different partial elements of truth. It is seen every day in poor human nature, so that I do not insist on this; but some I will refer to. Two of these witnesses—Rome and the early Church—disliked each other. Yet that dislike makes little impression upon us now. What an advance through indifferentism to an anti-Christian state ! For so absolute is truth, is Christ's claim, that " he that is not with me is against me." This dislike, that Dr. Temple and his school remain unaffected by, is the deadly persecuting hatred of Christians, of the saints (certainly, whatever faults there may have been, the excellent of the earth), by the heathens—the hatred of Christ and His people by the worshippers of idols and devils—the enmity of man and Satan (for we are not going to give up our belief that Jesus was the Christ of God for these gentlemen) against the Son of God and all that owned Him. This makes little impression on them, no doubt. In the fourth essay we read, " It was natural for a Christian in the earliest period to look upon the heathen state in which he found himself, as if it belonged to the kingdom of Satan, and not to that of God; and, consecrated as it was in all its offices to the heathen divinities, to consider it a society having its origin from the powers of darkness, not from the Lord of light and life." And what do these clergymen and professed teachers of Christianity believe ?

What were the heathen gods and goddesses ? I read in the first essay, " The natural religious shadows projected by the spiritual light within, showing on the dark problems without, were all in reality systems of law given also by God, though not given by revelation." No doubt, they say, they distorted and corrupted, etc. But can you for a moment believe that the worship of Jupiter, and Venus, and Bacchus, and horrors which are simple facts as they may be read in Romans i. (which after all, though in just language, passes over the surface of turpitude, not to defile itself by sinking into details I cannot here refer to either), were systems of law given by God ? The worship of passions and devils, gloating in the unutterable degradation of God's most wonderful creature, a system of law given of God!

And it is false as to its history. Heathenism was, even in this aspect, the departure under devilish influence from the knowledge of God: Noah had this; and they did not like to retain God in their knowledge, and God gave them up to dishonour themselves. They degraded God to a brute, and themselves to worse after. It never was a training parallel to, and contemporaneous with, that of the Hebrews—a system of law given of God, and then corrupted. There was the knowledge of the true God, and men gave it up—as far as the history of these dark ages can be traced, a system deliberately taken up in Babel, to leave God, and separated into two hostile branches:—the Sabæans, who did not go farther than taking fire as a representative of God, as the modern Parsees; and Ionism, a system of horrible wickedness and idolatry pervading India, Egypt, Phœnicia, and thence Greece, which made (possibly through Orpheus and the Cabiri, certainly in Hesiod and Homer) pretty poetry of it, and so passing on to Rome, and, I have little doubt, far and wide elsewhere, modified according to the spirit and character of nations—at any rate, in historically known nations, a common universal system.

It is a perfect iniquity to say as to the principle of it, and false as to the history of it, that these were systems of law given of God, though not by revelation. There was a knowledge of God departed from. This was corrupted, and man with it. Devils and deified passions took the place of God in the heart. To say, "Ultimately the gospel was to have sway in doing more perfectly that which heathen religions were doing imperfectly," has only to be stated to revolt every divinely taught mind. What did heathenism do? Hold the State together. Be it so; but they admit this only decorated the surface of it. But morally in relationship to God, what did it do? That these educators of the world do not, I suppose, care about. Christianity, they say, was not only to quicken the spirit of the individual (what is that?) but to sanctify civil institutions—heathenism decorated the surface. But even as to the Church, heathenism, they tell us, had its national churches.

This defence of heathenism seems to me, dear friend, as immoral in its character as it is false historically. In heathenism there was, as there must be in man, an instinct as to God, but laid hold of by Satan to pander to the passions of men—God, with some instinctive remains of a supreme God (*testimonium animæ naturaliter Christianæ*), turned into calves, cats, and monkeys, and beasts!

There were four principles, as it seems to me, at work in heathenism:—the instinct of a supreme Being, or a superior one, at any rate, above man, impossible to be got rid of; heroism, or the deification of ancestors, traceable everywhere, and connecting itself, in its earlier and oriental phases, with Noah and his family and the ark (the idea is carried to excess by Bryant, but it seems to me incontrovertible); thirdly, the stars, as something wonderful, instinct with movement, and acting on the earth; and lastly, what led to such horrible corruption, the sense of a generative power of nature, partly abstract, partly running through every sphere of thought and connected with the ruin of nature, and a certain resurrection of power, which linked it with day and night, and summer and winter. This, helped by various traditions, formed various systems; but all of man without God, to be found if at all, as the ἄγνωστος θεὸς—in India, in certain respects, the most elevated, but the most monstrous, more of God's interest in man and His coming down, though there was Apotheosis—in Egypt one more wise and applied to human morality and organization, yet the same system thoroughly, with more of the sentiment of a definite judgment of God, and conflict of good and evil, in the history of Osiris, Amenti, and Typhon, dead men not execrated were called justified—in Greece, the lowest and poorest of all, which made man and poetry everything (gods became men, or swans, or bulls, to indulge their passions). It was the deification of man, and morally more contemptible than all. No gods but gods of human passions, money, war, corrupt lusts—gods in which there was no single association with conscience, except a dreary Tartarus for those who might despise them, and an Elysium so poor that Achilles complained bitterly of being there. It is the system of the deification of human passions, and another world only used to make gods of them, and these gods, that is devils, important, and this world the only excellent place. This was a system of law we are told, given of God. I am silent. I fear I should be rebuked by you for something contemptuous and bitter, and say nothing of what I feel.

As to Rome there was nothing new, they were not poetical, but political; and their religion too. The god *Terminus* was immovable. Can these clergymen show me one single proof of any heathenism being a system of law given of God? The instinct that there is something above him is in man—cannot be eradicated : a conscience accompanies him, in spite of the devil. Is there anything to be found in heathenism besides this fact, perverted to men's offering the things which they offered to devils, and not to God; and the consecrating the worst passions, and their most intolerable effects to these devils or dung-gods, as Scripture calls them, so as to destroy that conscience, if it had been possible ? Do our Essayists think their judgment of heathenism, or that of Scripture in the Old and New Testament, the most correct ? Their admirable Trajan they must view as a heathen to admire. They turn round the other side, and see that the subduer of Dacia, the mighty emperor, is with heartless indifference of character the cool persecutor of those who owned the Son of God, and the restorer of sacrifices to devils. "They are so eager for light, that they will rub their eyes in the dark, and take the resulting optical delusions for real flashes." Excuse me: I quote this not very elegant image of Dr. Temple's, as a singular but not inapt description of a state of mind in which, of course, he has not described himself.

In fine, the foundation of the whole system is false. There was progress in the revelation of God's mind, because of the alienation of man from God, and the ignorance that was in him ; but it never was the education of the world at all. It began, not by law, but, as became the God of all grace, by promise, yet not by promise to the world, though in favour of it, and for all that should believe it at all times ; then law, yet not given to the world, but to a people separated out of it because of the horrible state the world was in, and a careful separation made between them to keep at any rate, in one little corner, the knowledge of the true God, that all might not be wholly debased ; then the Son of God coming into it, but the world knew Him not, His own received Him not, and they joined in crucifying Him. He was the Shepherd of a little flock. Then the Holy Ghost sent, whom the world cannot receive, because it seeth

Him not, neither knoweth Him; but given to those who believe; but with the fullest witness of grace to all who do believe the record God has given concerning His Son. Does Dr. Temple believe these facts, or deny them? Is he, that is, a Christian or an infidel?

Heathenism was not different contemporary systems of law given of God, but the giving up the knowledge of the true God, and plunging into devilish idolatry and bestial corruption, though God did not allow, let Satan do what he could, that they should destroy the instincts that there was a God, nor flee from the torment of a violated conscience. The whole system is historically and actually false. I believe, dear friend, in Christianity, not in the reveries of those who (to use their own somewhat vulgar simile already quoted, which I only do use as theirs) " are so eager for light [not having God's and reflecting it, Christ come as light into the world in darkness], that they will rub their eyes in the dark, and take the resulting optical delusions for real flashes." It suggests to me the word addressed to poor Israel on lower ground than ours, for the true light now shines: " Who is among you that feareth Jehovah, that obeyeth the voice of His servant, that walketh in darkness, and hath no light? let him trust in the name of Jehovah, and stay upon his God. Behold, all ye that kindle a fire, that compass yourselves about with sparks, walk in the light of your fire, and in the sparks that ye have kindled. This shall ye have at my hand; ye shall lie down in sorrow."

You know well, your heart knows, dear friend, how utterly far my spirit is from an ungracious feeling towards the authors of these essays, of whom I have no knowledge whatever, and desire unfeignedly from the bottom of my heart their good and blessing. But such is their path.

I speak of the system—a system so hard and unfeeling, that it has no idea but of beginning with law; that even a mother's tender care of the fruit of the womb is known only as correcting wilfulness of temper, and germs of wanton cruelty; that it sees no promise, no grace, but God beginning with a law to repress already ripened wickedness—a system which ignores the fall, yet sees only wanton cruelty and wilfulness of temper in an infant; and begins God's history after some two thousand five hundred years resulting in a plague of wickedness, to ignore the flood.

I believe in a revelation which contains an external law, brought in by the bye to test man, and show him what he was, but in a revelation of grace, life, redemption, the revelation of the Son of God, of God Himself, bringing down heavenly things which the human heart cannot spell out or divine if unrevealed; which brings a revealed God and light to man; and man, made fit for it by love, into the perfect light by redemption, and gives him a new nature capable of enjoying it, and soon (how soon One only knows) glory out of this world; a revelation through which (to close what I have to say in the blessed words of Scripture—how does it meet everything!) those who have received it, instead of learning from heathens, own in moral uprightness the ruin of the old man, and have put it off, " and have put on the new man, which is renewed in knowledge after the image of Him that created him; where there is neither Greek nor Jew, circumcision nor uncircumcision, Barbarian, Scythian, bond nor free; but Christ is all, and in all."

W. I am uncommonly glad I met you. The system is a judged one for me. It is not of God. It is evidently exalting man and heathenism at the expense of Christ. I

K

am not master of all the points to which you have referred, but I see enough to have the distinct conviction of the hollowness of the system, even as to facts. But how happy it is that the Scripture itself gives so fully all that is needed, not only to save, but to make a man wise unto salvation, through faith that is in Christ Jesus, and then thoroughly furnished unto all good works!

It must be distracting and defiling to wade through these mythological systems, with all their aberrations and pollutions, but, with the holy judgment of God, the word of God in a few short verses tells us all its history. How admirable this is; how evidently one sees the hand and Spirit of God in it! There certainly is a stamp in the word of God of what is Divine, which is unmistakable, even where it is most human.

H. In truth there is—a simplicity, a dignity: no one ever produced anything like it. You have only to read apocryphal books. There is effort in them; there is none in Scripture. Not once do you find an epithet attached to Jesus (that were a human feeling, perhaps a right one), but what He is to tell its own tale of what He is. What human writer, in recording His history, would have kept uniformly to this? Yet how it becomes a Divine person! Every epithet would lower. They may be put as the expression of my sentiment, but not as the cause of them. And how it has forced man to deal with it! Infidels or not, they must deal with it where it is. It is God telling us in grace, but telling us of Himself, telling of heavenly things, and for man. What can man do? It concerns him. He may be angry with the grace—angry to be forced to say he does not like what is heavenly, he may exalt heathenism which has been tired of itself; but there it is, and he has to say to it. Blessed they who have tasted that God is in it—speaks in it, and that have found Him to be holy, as He must be, but love in revealing Himself to them, and in bringing them by redemption and Divine righteousness to Himself to enjoy Him for ever! But we must part, dear friend, in the common enjoyment, I trust, of this hope.

W. Shall we not meet again, and take these questions up? There are more of these Essays, and we may find means, through God's grace, to get profit in weighing them in the light, particularly as these questions are current.

H. Perhaps God may permit it to be so. We have gone over, I believe, the fundamental questions as to it. I am, as you know, constantly occupied with more direct work. Yet I fully recognise the importance of these subjects. These Essays, which seem to me very superficial, are but the sign of a state of feeling of a large class, or they would not be worth notice. It is an effort of Satan to pervert and really heathenize the country, and swamp revealed religion. It is going on everywhere in Christendom. The attempted counteraction of ordinances, whether Stahl and Hengstenberg in Germany, or what is called Puseyism in England, cannot meet the wants of a soul, even though there may be personal piety, which is anything but required for that system. In France it is the ultramontane system, which is the counterbalance. In the feeble Protestantism which is there, there is none. It is infidelity, or the new evangelical party infected with rationalism, with many individually pious persons. But I shall see you, and, if leisure permits me, will take up any further questions that may occur.

I would refer you in parting—you who do believe in the word of God—to 1 John v. where the exactly opposite

view to Dr. Temple on every point is given. For this is
the will of God, that we keep His commandments. There
is obedience to a commandment, the proof of love; and
His commandments are not grievous. For whatsoever
is born of God overcometh the world. There is a new
nature, and the world not educated, but overcome. Who
is he that overcometh the world, but he that believeth
that Jesus is the Son of God? There is faith on a perfect
external revealed object, the only means of obtaining the
victory. At the end of 1 John iii. you will find, as in
Romans viii., the Spirit, the Holy Ghost given, carefully
distinguished from the spirit or conscience within. Christianity is a deliverance sent by God to form the spirit
according to a new life on an object supremely blessed
without, so as to take out of self, and fix the heart on
that supreme object of blessedness. Dr. Temple's or the
rationalist's system is a rejection of it, for the spirit or
fallen nature of man to form itself by heathenism and
Christianity as pretty nearly on a par, the latter being
reduced by him to within a shade of the level of the
former.

If you would have blessing or holy and Divine affections, hold fast the revelation of a Divine object, and the
Divine revelation of that object.

Butler & Tanner, The Selwood Printing Works, Frome, and London.

www.ingramcontent.com/pod-product-compliance
Lightning Source LLC
LaVergne TN
LVHW061218060426
835508LV00014B/1348